Presented to:

· ·

by:

· ·

date:

· ·

Surely your goodnesss and love will be with me all my life.
—Psalm 23:6

First published in the USA 2003 by Kregel
Publications, a division of Kregel, Inc.,
P.O. Box 2607, Grand Rapids, MI 49501.
Kregel Publications provides trusted,
biblical publications for Christian growth
and service. Your comments and
suggestions are valued.

Edited by Tim Dowley
Designed by Peter Wyart,
Three's Company

Worldwide coedition organized and
produced by Angus Hudson Ltd,
Concorde House,
Grenville Place, Mill Hill,
London NW7 3SA, England
Tel: +44 20 8959 3668
Fax: +44 20 8959 3678

ISBN 0-8254-2044-x

Printed in Singapore
1 2 3 4 5 / 07 06 05 04 03

BEGINNING WITH GOD

BEGINNING WITH GOD

Steve T. Barclift

ILLUSTRATIONS BY
TONY KENYON

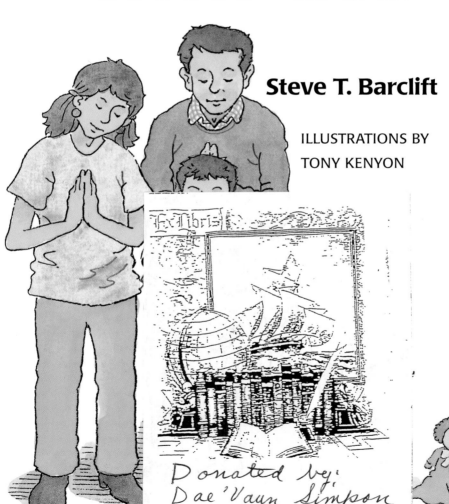

For my children:
Wesley, Elaina, Angela, and Hannah.

And for my wife, Jann.

I love you all very much.

Introduction

Welcome to *Beginning with God.* This book contains fifty-two fun and interesting units—enough to enjoy one per week for a whole year!

There are thirteen weekly units for each of the four seasons (fall, winter, spring, and summer), and you can turn to whatever season it is now and get started.

The weekly devotions are set up so you can do them on your own. But you may want to get your whole family involved—either in doing the whole unit or maybe just certain parts. (For example, each week there is a fun activity that is great to do as a family.) Each unit is divided into six parts. You can pick a time once each week to sit down and read all six parts at once, or you may want to follow a schedule something like this:

Sunday: Read the story that begins the unit.

Monday: Answer the questions in the section called "**Check Your Head for What You've Read.**"

Tuesday: Take your Bible and follow the instructions in the section "**A Look Inside God's Special Book.**"

Wednesday: Learn the Scripture in the section "**Let's Rehearse a Bible Verse.**"

Thursday: Focus on praying as you follow the suggestions under "**When You Pray, Day by Day.**"

Friday or Saturday: Try out the activities in the section called "**Something Fun for Everyone.**"

Of course you can combine these different parts in other ways too—in whatever way is best for you. The important thing is simply to read and enjoy them, and along the way to learn more about God and the Bible and yourself and others.

There also is another way to use *Beginning with God.* As things that confuse or trouble you come up during the week, look in the "*Topics and Stories Index*" in the back of the book. Suppose you're having a problem with temptation. By looking up "*temptation*" in the index, you quickly find the pages in this book that offer answers to your questions.

May this be the beginning of a lifetime of enjoying regular devotional times with God!

FALL

September
October
November

Thanksgiving Day
(Week 12)

A New Family on the Block
Learning to be a good neighbor

"Mom! Dad!" yelled Johnny to his parents as he leapt over a flower bed onto the front porch. "Someone's moving into that old house on the corner!"

Johnny's sisters, Elaina and Joy, sat on the porch steps, brushing their dollies' hair.

"It's about time," said Father. "That house has been empty all year. I only hope they'll cut down those awful weeds growing in the yard!"

"Let's go welcome the new family to our neighborhood," suggested Mother.

Together the Kenton family walked down the street. At the end of the block, they saw a moving van. It had been backed up to the porch of a very old house with peeling paint.

"Mommy, those people don't take very good care of their things," Elaina said as two men carried a worn-out couch off the moving van.

"Their truck is ugly too," added Joy, pointing to an old, dented van parked at the curb. The van's back doors were open, and clothes, toys, and scraps of paper could be seen scattered about inside.

"I'm not sure I'll like these people," said Johnny. "Their truck is a mess."

Father looked at his children. "I don't think we've made a very good start at welcoming our new neighbors, have we, kids?" asked Father. "We've said bad things about them because they're moving into a house that needs work, their furniture is old, and their van isn't pretty and is messy after their trip. Is that how Jesus would treat a new family on *His* block?"

The children looked down and slowly shook their heads. They were sorry for their unkind thoughts and words.

11

"How can we welcome them in a way that would make Jesus happy?" asked Johnny.

No one spoke for a few moments.

"Well, I'm going to make sandwiches and lemonade for them and all of us," said Mother. "They may be hungry and thirsty after their trip."

"I'll help!" added Joy, who was learning to be Mommy's helper around the house.

"I guess I'll ask if they'd like help with anything— like cleaning out their van, maybe," said Johnny quietly.

"And I'll see if they'd like to come to church with us tomorrow!" announced Elaina.

Let's Rehearse a Bible Verse

It is a sin to hate your neighbor.
But being kind to the needy
brings happiness.
Proverbs 14:21

"Those are good ideas, kids," said Dad, smiling.
"After the moving van is empty, I'm going to offer
to mow down all these ugly weeds!"

Just then a woman pushing a boy in a wheelchair
came out on the porch. Another boy, who looked
to be about Johnny's age, followed her out the
door. The woman waved and smiled.

"Well, what are we waiting for?" said Mother.
"Let's go welcome our new neighbors!"

Check Your Head for What You've Read

1. Were the Kenton children being good neighbors when they said unkind things about the new family on their block?

2. Did the new family's old house, dented and messy van, and worn furniture mean they weren't nice people? Why not?

3. Why should we try to be good neighbors?

A Look Inside God's Special Book

Jesus once told a story about a man who was beat up and robbed by some bad men. They left him in the road to die. Two men from the man's own country came by and looked at him. But they didn't stop to help.

Do you know what happened next? A man from a foreign country came by and helped the man! So who was the good neighbor in this story?

You can find this story in Luke 10.

When You Pray, Day by Day
Ask God:
- to show you how to be a good neighbor
- to protect and care for poor people
- to help you meet people you can help.

Thank Jesus for being your special Friend.

Something Fun for Everyone
If a new family moves to your neighborhood, here are some ways to show them Christ's love by making them feel welcome.

• **Host a "You Are Welcome" party for the new family**. For example, if the Brown family has just moved in nearby, make a banner proclaiming a "Brown Family Appreciation Day." Supply goodies—such as cookies and punch or fruit juice—and help the new people get to know your family.

• **Take the new family a bouquet of flowers and a hand-drawn map of the neighborhood**. Show on the map where you live, where other neighbors live, and the location of schools, stores in the area, churches, the nearest hospital, and the public library. Draw on the map everything you can think of that might help someone new be happy in your neighborhood.

Hint: Even if you have no new neighbors, take flowers or cookies to a person or family nearby who might need to know that someone loves them.

Someone Special Needs a Friend
Being the friend of a special-needs child

The Smiths and Kentons were enjoying a "moving-day picnic" of sandwiches and lemonade in the Smiths' living room. Stacks of boxes and pieces of old furniture were all around them.

Mrs. Smith said she had moved here to take a job as the office manager of a small business. The job wouldn't pay well, she explained, but it was a new beginning for her family.

Johnny and Caleb, Mrs. Smith's oldest son, each ate a sandwich while they played teeter-totter on a board balanced across the top of a wooden box. It was a noisy and bumpy ride. Elaina sat on the floor nearby, quietly playing with the Smiths' fuzzy orange kitten.

Joy was busy unpacking a big box full of toys. She carefully put each toy into the empty drawers of a chest that was *supposed* to be for Caleb's clothes. But no one seemed to mind.

Eli Smith sat in a wheelchair by his mother's side. His head slowly wobbled from side to side as his mother talked.

"I'm worried about Eli," said Mrs. Smith. "He will be in the first grade at Thompson Elementary, but he doesn't know any children here yet."

"Elaina is in the first grade at Thompson this year too," said Father. "Who is Eli's teacher?"

"Miss Corsack," answered Mrs. Smith.

"That's *my* teacher!" said Elaina, suddenly interested. Eli's eyes seemed to brighten at this news.

17

"Maybe Elaina could introduce Eli to some of the other children," Mother suggested. "What do you think, Elaina?"

Elaina wrinkled her nose and made a funny face. "I . . . I don't know," she finally said. "I don't think I want to." She looked down at the kitten and said nothing more.

As she tucked Elaina into bed that night, Mother asked Elaina why she did not want to help Eli.

"Mommy, I'd like to help, but Eli is . . . *different* from other kids. He rolls his head around all the time, and he can't feed himself. He talks funny, too. And sometimes he drools like a baby. I don't know how to help someone like that."

"Elaina," began Mother, "sometimes Jesus wants us to do things that aren't easy for us to do on our own. We do them out of love—*Christ's* love.

18

"Did you know Eli can see, hear, and think just like you can? His mommy says Eli can play games and have fun with other children. All he needs is a special friend who is willing to help. Will you be Eli's friend?"

"Mommy, do you think I can be?" asked Elaina. "Will I know how to help him?"

"I'm sure you can do it, sweetie, if that's what you really want. Should we ask Jesus for *His* help?"

Elaina nodded and smiled as Mother knelt beside the bed to pray with her.

Let's Rehearse a Bible Verse

Forgive each other just as God forgave you in Christ.

Ephesians 4:32

Check Your Head for What You've Read

1. Why didn't Elaina want to help Eli meet people at his new school?

2. When Elaina said she wouldn't help, how do you think Eli felt?

3. Do you think Jesus loves people who are different from us? Should we love them too?

A Look Inside God's Special Book

Do you know the story of Jonah? God told Jonah to go to a faraway city and tell the people there to stop doing the bad things they were doing. But Jonah did not want to go. Instead, he got aboard a ship and tried to run away from God.

So what did God do? He sent a giant fish to swallow Jonah in one big gulp! Inside the stomach of the fish, Jonah had a change of heart. He prayed that God would forgive him, and he promised to do what God asked if he could get out of the belly of the fish.

God answered Jonah's prayer. He made the fish spit Jonah out. And with God's help, Jonah was able to do what God had told him to do.

Look for this story in the book of Jonah in the Bible.

When You Pray, Day by Day
Ask God:

• to help you understand the needs and feelings of people who are different from you

• to show you how to love and help people who have special needs.

Thank God for bringing people into your life who love and help you.

Something Fun for Everyone

Do you know someone who must spend most of his time in a wheelchair? Be a friend to that person. When you get together, try doing some of these things:

• **Take along a portable CD player or tape player and play some of your favorite music**. Play some of your friend's favorite music, too.

• **Read storybooks aloud and show any pictures on the pages to your friend**. Many storybooks are available on CD, cassette tape, or in CD-and-book or tape-and-book combinations. These are great to share.

• **Play "Build and Destroy."** Construct tall buildings out of wood blocks and let your friend knock them down. Many children who have limited use of their arms can do this and usually love it!

Remember: Whenever you can introduce your friend to someone else, please do—meeting others can be difficult for children with special needs.

The Kentons Have a Meeting

Sharing

It was Sunday afternoon, and Joy and Mother had just cleared away the lunch dishes.

"Kids, Daddy and I want to have a family meeting. Let's all gather around the table for a few minutes," suggested Mother.

"But Dad and I were going to play catch," said Johnny.

"Our meeting won't last long," Father answered.

Mother handed Johnny a wet rag so he could wipe the table clean.

"Daddy and I have been praying about something important, and we need to talk to you children about it," said Mother as she poured juice for everyone.

"Business has not been good at our store," began Father. Mr. Kenton owned a small hardware shop. "The new shopping center in town has taken some of our customers. So it has become hard to pay our bills."

"And God wants us to pay people for the things we buy from them," added Mother. "So to help out, I will be starting a new job this week."

"A job? What kind of job, Mother?" asked Johnny.

"Young children sometimes need to stay with someone who will take good care of them while their parents work. I'll take care of some of those children right here at home," Mother explained.

23

"Tell us what you think of all this, kids," said Father.

Each of the children looked confused and a little sad.

> **Let's Rehearse a Bible Verse**
>
> God loves the person who gives happily.
>
> 2 Corinthians 9:7

"If Mommy takes care of other kids here at our house, does that mean they will get to play with all our toys?" asked Elaina.

"We make God happy when we share," said Mother. "We have lots of family toys that we can share with the children I take care of. But each of you has special toys that we will not ask you to share. And I'll make sure the children take good care of our family toys."

"Mommy," began four-year-old Joy quietly, "will you still have time to play with *me?*"

Mother looked at Joy and smiled. "Honey, I'll *always* find a way to make time for you. I love each of my children so very much.

"Did you know that God loves each of us too? The Bible says Jesus knows all about our problems and the things we need. He wants to take care of us. But we must talk to Him about our needs."

"What do you think we should do right now, kids?" asked Father.

"We need to pray," said Johnny. His sisters nodded their heads up and down.

"That's what I think too," Father agreed. "Let's thank Jesus for showing us how to pay our bills, and ask Him to help Mommy and our family as Mommy starts her new job."

Check Your Head for What You've Read

1. What news did Mother and Father share with the children at the family meeting?

2. What was Elaina afraid might happen if Mother cared for other children in the Kentons' home? Is it important for us to be willing to share?

3. How do the Kenton children know God loves and will care for them?

A Look Inside God's Special Book

Do you know the Bible story about a boy who took five loaves of bread and two fish with him when he went to hear Jesus talk? Enough people to fill a town had gathered to hear Jesus, but this boy was the only one who brought food to eat!

Do you remember what happened? The boy gave the bread and fish to Jesus. Jesus thanked God for the food and split it up so that all the people had plenty of food and there was lots left over. What a wonderful story about sharing!

Find this story in Matthew 14; Mark 6; Luke 9; and John 6.

When You Pray, Day by Day
Ask God:
• to help you be happy to share with others
• for protection when you are not with your parents.
Thank God for loving you and for wanting to provide
for your needs.

Something Fun for Everyone
Have you ever gotten excited about a Bible story you
have heard or read and wanted to share that story with
someone? Here are a couple of fun ways to do just that!
• **Make paper-bag puppets**. You can make Bible character
puppets by drawing faces on paper lunch bags. Use bright-
colored marking pens for faces and clothes, and cut out
 eyes. Or glue colored construction paper to the bags for hair,
beards, eyebrows, eyes, and clothing. Then use the puppets
to act out the story.
• **Make puppets-on-a-stick.** Glue some of the pictures
from old Sunday school papers to pieces of cardboard.
Cut out the figures of people in the pictures.
Then glue a Popsicle stick to the back of each figure,
near the bottom (for a handle). Use these stick
puppets to help you tell the Bible story.
Hint: Don't forget to make animal puppets too.
Animals are often important Bible characters!

An Incident at School
Forgiveness

"Eli is a dum-my. Nanny nanny naaan-neee," said Jeremy on the playground at school.

I . . . I am *n-not* a dum . . . a d-dummy," answered Eli. Several boys and girls laughed at the boy in a wheelchair who had trouble saying his words.

"That's right, Jeremy Brown!" said Elaina. "He *isn't* a dummy!" It was recess time at school, and Elaina had taken Eli outside so he could enjoy the fall sunshine.

"He is so," said Jeremy. "Just look at him—he can't hold his head up right, and he drools like my baby brother."

"He can't help doing those things and you know it!" answered Elaina. "Leave him alone!"

Laughing together, the unkind children went away to play.

"I'm sorry they were mean to you, Eli," said Elaina. "Please don't feel bad."

"Th . . . th . . . they were right. I am a d-dummy," he answered. "T . . . take me back inside." Tears were running down Eli's cheeks.

When she got home from school, Elaina told Mother what had happened on the playground that day. Mother had just finished dressing the three-year-old Bradley twins in clean clothes. The two busy boys had gotten dirty digging holes in one of Mother's flower beds.

"I was so mad, Mommy!" said Elaina. "I wanted to say bad things to Jeremy and to hurt him for talking that way to Eli."

"Elaina, it's right to hurt for Eli when others tease him. You saw how Jeremy's mean words made Eli feel bad about himself, and it made you very angry. God gave you your feeling of anger, and when you keep anger in control, it's good.

"But God also wants us to do a very hard thing. Rather than strike out at people who are cruel to us and to our friends, Jesus wants us to *forgive* them. And He wants us to love them, too."

Elaina didn't speak right away. She was thinking about Mother's words.

"Mommy," Elaina finally said, "I think I *can* forgive Jeremy and the others for being mean. They don't know Eli very well, and maybe they didn't know how unhappy their words and laughing made him feel.

"But, Mommy," continued Elaina, "I don't think I can ever *love* them."

"Maybe you can't on your own, honey," said Mother. "But with Jesus' help, you can learn to love them."

"Really?" said Elaina. "Jesus can do that?"

"Yes, Elaina," answered Mother. "He can and He will–if you ask Him to."

"Then that's what I'm going to do," said Elaina with a smile.

Mother put her arm around Elaina and pulled her close. "I'm proud of you, sweetie. I love you very much."

"I love you too, Mommy," Elaina said.

Check Your Head for What You've Read

1. Why was Elaina mad at Jeremy and the other children on the playground?

2. Is teasing another person *always* wrong? When *is* it wrong to tease someone?

3. What should we do when it's hard to forgive and love a person?

A Look Inside God's Special Book

If you ever have a hard time forgiving someone, think about the story of Joseph.

Joseph had eleven brothers. His older brothers hated Joseph because he was their father's favorite son. The jealous brothers sold Joseph to slave traders. He became a slave in the faraway land of Egypt.

God helped Joseph become an important ruler in Egypt, but Joseph's brothers didn't know this. They went to Egypt to try to buy food. When he saw his brothers, do you think Joseph sent them away? No! He gave them food and welcomed them with love. Joseph forgave his brothers.

The story of Joseph can be found in Genesis 37–45.

When You Pray, Day by Day
Ask God:
• to help you know when your teasing (or someone else's) may hurt someone
• to show you how to forgive and love people who do wrong things to you or someone you know.
Thank God for loving you and for wanting to forgive your sins.

Something Fun for Everyone
Have you ever been teased? If you have, your feelings may have been hurt. Maybe your brother or sister, or someone at school, has borrowed something from you without asking, and damaged it. If so, how did that make you feel?

When someone does something bad to us, we often become angry and want to "get even"—to do something bad to that person in return. It's not easy to do, but God wants us to forgive those who do bad things to us.

Make an "I Forgive You" card. Fold a sheet of white paper or construction paper in half, making the fold in the paper's long sides. Next, carefully fold the already folded paper one more time. You now have a blank card. Open the card. On the inside, write a kind note to a person who did something bad to you, telling the person that you forgive him or her. Using markers, crayons, or water colors, make a pretty picture on the outside of the card. Then give the card to the person.

People react in different ways when we forgive them—some are thankful, some are not. But even when your mercy isn't well received, offering it is always good for your heart; you will be happier, and God will be pleased with you.

Johnny Runs for Class President

Honesty

"Are you running for classroom president, Johnny?" asked his best friend, Champion.

"Yup!" answered Johnny.

"Hey, that's great!" said Champion. "Can I be your campaign manager?"

"You're on!" said Johnny.

"I hear Kyle is running too," said Champion.

33

"Yes," answered Johnny. "That's what Mr. Bentley said." Mr. Bentley–who was usually called "Mr. B"–was the boys' teacher at school.

"I don't think Kyle has a chance," said Champion. "He's a showoff and a troublemaker. I doubt many kids will vote for him."

The next day at school, Mr. Bentley talked about the rules for running for classroom president.

"Most important of all," he said, "I want our candidates to agree to run honest, friendly campaigns. You'll both get a chance to share your ideas with the class before the election next Monday."

Johnny and Champion worked hard all that week. They made posters and told classmates why they thought Johnny should be president.

"This has been a lot of work," said Johnny as he and Champion hung a poster in the hall.

"You can say *that* again," answered Champion. "Have you noticed that Kyle hasn't done much to get ready for the election? And he just goofed off when he had his chance to speak to the class."

"Yes, I've wondered about that," said Johnny. "I guess he doesn't really care about winning."

On Monday morning, Mr. B had all the students put the name of their candidate on a piece of paper and drop it into a shoe box.

"OK, class—I'll count the ballots now and see who our president will be," said Mr. B. "Kyle has thirteen votes . . . and Johnny has twelve. Congratulations, Kyle!"

After school, as Johnny and Champion walked slowly toward home, a boy came running after them.

"Hey, guys! Wait for me!" he shouted.

"Hi, Robbie," said Johnny.

"I've got something to tell you," said Robbie. "It's about the election."

"The election is *old* news," said Champion.

"Just *listen!*" Robbie pleaded. "Kyle cheated. He gave a dollar to everyone he could get to vote for him."

Robbie looked down at the sidewalk. "He bought my vote too. I'm sorry."

35

"I think *we* should have cheated," said Champion. "We would have won if we had."

"It isn't right to cheat," said Johnny.

"Right?" said Champion. "We're talking about winning and losing, Johnny! We played fair and lost the election. Kyle cheated—and he won."

"In God's eyes we *didn't* lose," said Johnny. "The Bible says it's wrong to cheat. We make God happy when we're honest."

"I don't know much about God," said Champion. "We don't talk about Him at my house. Can you tell me more about Him?"

Johnny smiled. "You bet I can, friend."

36

Check Your Head for What You've Read

1. Why wasn't Kyle working very hard at his campaign for classroom president?
2. Johnny and Kyle both agreed to run honest campaigns. Why did Kyle break his promise?
3. Is cheating OK if it helps you win? What does the Bible say about being honest?

A Look Inside God's Special Book

The Bible tells the story of how Jacob tricked his blind old father, Isaac. Before he died, Isaac wanted to bless Jacob's older brother, Esau. So with his mother's help, Jacob set out to make his father think *Jacob* was Esau. He wanted to do this so *he* would receive their father's blessing.

But there was a problem. Esau liked to hunt, and he had thick, woolly hair all over his body. Jacob didn't. So Jacob put on his brother's hunting clothes and put sheepskins on his arms and neck. His father Isaac smelled the clothes and felt the sheepskins. Believing Jacob was Esau, Isaac asked God to bless his son and make him a leader of nations. Jacob stole his brother's blessing!

Read about Jacob in Genesis 27.

When You Pray, Day by Day
Ask God:
• to give you the courage to say no to the temptation to cheat
• to show you how to bring honor to Him in everything you do.
Thank God for giving you the Bible and the Holy Spirit to help you live as you should.

Something Fun for Everyone
The temptation to cheat, or to be dishonest in some other way, is something we face again and again. But God wants us to live a life that honors Him.

Make a Book of Honor. On sheets of construction paper, glue pictures of Bible characters, famous Christians, and other Christians who have led lives that honored God. For example, you might find a picture of John the Baptist in an old Sunday school paper, and a picture of a missionary in a missions magazine. In family photo albums you may be able to find pictures of grandparents who have honored God. Glue each picture on a sheet of construction paper. After you have several pictures for your book, add one more—a picture of *you*.

Staple the pages, or use a hole punch and string or yarn to tie them together. Write "My Book of Honor" on the front of the book, and look through it often to remind you of the obedient, godly lives of those pictured inside.

Winning Fair and Square
When telling isn't tattling

"Kyle and Johnny, I'd like to talk to both of you," said Mr. B at the end of class Tuesday. "The rest of the class is dismissed.

"Come up here, boys," Mr. B said as the last student walked out the door. "I've learned there was some cheating in yesterday's election."

39

"You must have squealed!" Kyle said to Johnny.

"No," said Mr. B, "Johnny didn't tell me. Some of your other classmates did.

"Kyle, you cheated to win the election. You also helped several of your classmates do something dishonest. What do you have to say for yourself?"

"Well, it's no big deal or anything," said Kyle. "It's not like it was a *real* election."

"You're wrong, Kyle," answered his teacher. "This *is* a big deal. We're trying to learn how to be good citizens in this class. You've shown us how dishonesty can hurt people."

Mr. B paused for a moment, then continued.

"Kyle, you must pay a price for cheating. Johnny will be declared winner of the election tomorrow, and you will apologize to your classmates for what you have done. I will be talking to your parents about this incident. I also will speak with the parents of each child who accepted your bribe. You can go home now, Kyle."

Kyle quietly left the room.

"Johnny, I'm a little disappointed in you too," said Mr. B.

"Why?" asked Johnny. "What did I do wrong?"

"You ran an honest campaign, Johnny," his teacher answered. "But you found out yesterday about Kyle's cheating, and you didn't come tell me about it today."

Johnny glanced away. "I was afraid to. I didn't think I should tattle, Mr. B," he said.

"There sometimes is a thin line between unnecessary tattling and telling adults about a serious problem that needs attention, Johnny," said Mr. B.

"When you know that a child is hurting someone, hurting something, or hurting himself, then it's your responsibility to share what you know with an adult."

Let's Rehearse a Bible Verse

Happy are the people who keep his rules.
They ask him for help with their whole heart.

Psalm 119:2

"But Kyle didn't hurt anyone, Mr. B," said Johnny.

"That's not true," his teacher answered. "He hurt you. You worked hard but lost the election unfairly. Kyle also hurt several other classmates by helping them do something dishonest.

"Kyle hurt himself, too. Right now you children are forming habits that may be with you all your life. I hope his parents and I can help Kyle before it becomes too difficult for him to change."

"I'm sorry I was afraid to speak up, Mr. Bentley," said Johnny.

Mr. B put his hand on Johnny's shoulder and smiled. "You'll do better next time," he said. "And congratulations for winning the election, Johnny! You won it fair and square."

Check Your Head for What You've Read

1. What did Kyle do that hurt other people? How did he hurt himself?

2. What did Johnny do that was wrong? Why didn't he want to tell about Kyle's cheating?

3. Does it matter to God if you don't speak up when you should? How can you get God's help?

A Look Inside God's Special Book

Doing the right thing isn't always easy. Moses once got into trouble in Egypt and ran away to another country. While he was in that country, God spoke to him from a burning bush that did not burn up. God told Moses to go back to Egypt and tell Pharaoh to let the Hebrew people go. They were slaves there. God had seen their suffering and wanted them to be free again.

Moses was afraid to go to Pharaoh. He was certain he couldn't convince Pharaoh to let the Hebrew people go. But God told Moses He would be with him and help him. Moses trusted God, and with God's help, he led the Hebrew people out of slavery and on to the Promised Land. We can trust God to help us do what is right!

Read more about this story in Exodus 3–4.

43

When You Pray, Day by Day
Ask God:
• to help you know when to tell an adult you think someone is doing something wrong
• to know how to be a good citizen at school, in your town, and of your country.

Thank God for being there to help you do what's right.

Something Fun for Everyone

Do you sometimes find it hard to tell your parents or teacher when someone is doing something that you think is wrong, because you're afraid you will be tattling? At times it is very important to speak to an adult about another child's bad behavior; the difficult thing is knowing when to speak up.

Make an "I Will Tell When . . ." List. Ask a parent or another adult to meet with you to discuss when it is appropriate to tell an adult that someone you know has done something wrong. (If you have any siblings, it may be best to have them present for the discussion.)

Together, make a list with the heading at the top, "I Will Tell When . . ." Write down things that you and your parent or other adult agree should be on the list. For example, if you know someone is taking medicine not given to him or her by a parent, tell an adult. Is someone you know being a bully to you or another child? Tell an adult. Maybe you know someone who is hurting animals. Doing that is wrong; add it to your list. You also should tell an adult if you know someone who is stealing or cheating on tests.

After you complete the list, display it on a bulletin board or somewhere else in your bedroom, where you will see it regularly.

Remember: Telling an adult is always the right thing to do when you see a person hurting someone, something, or himself or herself.

Is the Christian Life Boring?

Having fun as a Christian

Elaina quietly came in the front door. She took off her backpack and coat and went into the kitchen to look for her mother.

"Oh! Hi, Elaina," said Mother. "I didn't hear you come in." She looked at Elaina. "You seem kind of sad, sweetie. Is something wrong?"

45

Elaina watched as Mother poured flour and other ingredients into a big bowl. Joy began stirring the mixture with a wooden spoon.

"Mommy," said Elaina, "is it true that Christians aren't supposed to have fun?"

"Why do you ask that, Elaina?" Mother asked.

"Well," she began, "when I told a boy in my class that my family is Christian, he said he feels sorry for me. He said God doesn't want Christians to have fun. Is that true?"

"Let's put our cake on to bake and we'll talk about it," said Mother.

Joy and Elaina sat down on the couch with Mother.

"Christians have some very good reasons to be happy and have fun," began Mother. "Let's take a look at what the Bible says.

"In the book of Matthew, in chapter five, Jesus says we should try to be happy when people say bad things about us, because we have a lot to look forward to in heaven."

"Mommy, I know heaven will be nice," said Elaina. "But we might not go to heaven for a long time. Is it bad to be happy and have fun *now?*"

"Let's look at another place in the Bible," said Mother. "In Philippians 4:4, Paul says, 'Be full of joy in the Lord always. I will say again, be full of joy.' Isn't Paul saying it's good for Christians to be happy?"

"Yes. . . . Well, I think so," Elaina said. "But does the Bible ever *show* anyone having fun?"

"Oh yes, Elaina," said Mother. "Let's find an example. Here's one in Nehemiah 12. God's people had just rebuilt the broken walls of Jerusalem. The Bible says they celebrated with shouts of joy, musical instruments, and singing.

"In verse 43 we read, 'They were happy because God made them very happy. The women and children were happy. The sound of happiness in Jerusalem could be heard far away.'"

"Wow! Reading about the fun God's people were having makes *me* happy," said Elaina.

"Should we do something fun as a family tonight, girls?" asked Mother.

"Let's have a party!"
suggested Joy.

"A let's-be-goofy party!"
added Elaina. "Can we have
cake and ice cream for
dinner tonight?"

"With lots of caramel topping!" said Joy.

"And can we have pizza—without onions or green peppers,
of course—for dessert?" asked Elaina. "Then can we sing songs,
and play games, and have a talent show before we go to bed?"

"I'd planned to have a casserole for dinner tonight, and read
you kids a book," answered Mother. "But we're Christians,
and it's Friday night—so let's have fun!"

Check Your Head for What You've Read

1. Why did Elaina think Christians were not supposed to have fun?
2. Who made God's people happy after they had rebuilt the walls of Jerusalem?
3. Where can we go to find answers about things in life that we don't understand?

A Look Inside God's Special Book

Jesus told a story about a young man who thought living a life that pleased God wasn't much fun. So he took his share of his father's money and went looking for good times in a faraway country. He wasted all his money on bad things, then found himself without friends, food, or a place to live.

The young man went to his father's house to ask if he could be a servant there. He was sorry for all the bad things he'd done. Do you know what happened? His father welcomed him with love, dressed him in fine clothes, and threw a big party for him! The young man now understood that living a life that pleased God was the right thing to do and could be lots of fun!

You can find this story in Luke 15:11–32.

When You Pray, Day by Day
Ask God:

• to show you how to have God's happiness in your heart

• to help make you aware of the good life you have as a Christian.

Thank God that Christians really *can* have more and better fun than people who don't know Jesus.

Something Fun for Everyone

To help you enjoy the good gift of joy that God has given you, set aside one night this week as a Family Fun Night.

• **Have a kitchen band.** Use an empty oatmeal box for a drum, and wooden spoons for drumsticks. The lids of pans make great cymbals (but Mom and Dad may want to plug their ears!). Bundles of jar rings held together with string sound like bells. And the handles of wooden spoons can be pounded together. Now make a joyful noise before the Lord!

• **Have a family talent show**. Each family member can dress up in any crazy way he wants and sing a song, lip-sync a song to recorded music, play an instrument, or perform magic tricks. Record the talent show on audio tape or videotape for more fun later on!

Remember: People who love Jesus have every reason to be the happiest people in the world.

Leaf Grief
Helping the elderly

"Kids, come here for a minute, please," Father called from the back porch. Johnny, Joy, and Elaina came running in from the backyard.

"What's up, Dad?" asked Johnny.

"I just had a call from Pastor Halperin," he answered. "Ralph and Virginia White, an elderly couple in our neighborhood, need to have their leaves raked up. I told Pastor Halperin we would help them today."

"But, Dad, it's Saturday!" moaned Johnny. "Champion and I were planning to get some guys together to play a game of football!"

"And Trina is going to come over to play jump rope," added Elaina.

"I'll help, Daddy," said Joy as she cradled Suzy, her favorite dolly, in her arms.

"Thanks, honey," said Father.

Johnny was not about to give up easily. "We *always* have to work on Saturday," he said. "It seems like we never get to play anymore."

Elaina nodded her head in agreement.

"I'm not pleased with your attitudes, kids," said Father. "If we all pitch in, this job will last only a couple of hours. God loves elderly people very much. We need to do the same. If you and Elaina won't help the Whites, then your mother, sister, and I will do it without you."

Johnny and Elaina looked a little embarrassed.

"I'm sorry, Daddy," said Elaina. "I'll help."

"Uh, yeah . . . me too, Dad," said Johnny. "I'll tell Champion we can't get together today."

"Thanks, kids," said Father. "Canceling with your friends may not be necessary though. Raking leaves can be fun. Maybe your friends would like to join us."

After lunch, the Kentons, Champion, and Trina met Virginia and Ralph White, then went to work.

They raked the leaves into tall piles, then the children took turns jumping into them. Sometimes they would completely disappear! The Whites and Mother and Father laughed as the

children played.
Finally, they put the
leaves into plastic bags
and stacked them by
the street.

Let's Rehearse a Bible Verse

God is fair. He will not forget the work you did
and the love you showed for him by helping his people.

Hebrews 6:10

"We just can't tell
you how much we appreciate your help," said Virginia White.

"That's right," added Ralph. "Say, I hear you boys like
football. I played football when I was young."

"Football was around when *you* were a boy, Mr. White?"
asked Champion.

"Oh, yes," answered Ralph with a chuckle.

"Ralph was a star player when he was in college," added
Mrs. White with a smile. "Let's go inside and warm up with
some hot apple cider and doughnuts. We can talk about
football!"

"Wow!" whispered Johnny to his father. "The
Whites are really cool. I'm glad we're getting to
know them."

"You kids are pretty cool too," Father whispered
back.

As they walked toward the house, Johnny felt
warm and happy inside.

Check Your Head for What You've Read

1. What was Pastor Halperin's call to Father about?

2. Did all the Kenton children want to help Mr. and Mrs. White at first? Why not?

3. How did the children help show Jesus' love to the Whites? How do you think helping the Whites made the children feel?

A Look Inside God's Special Book

Elisha traveled a lot and worked hard for God. In his travels he often passed through the town of Shunem. A good woman in that town wanted to help Elisha do God's work. One day she thought of a way to do that. The woman suggested to her husband that they fix up a small room for Elisha on their roof. From then on, whenever Elisha came to town he had a nice place to stay.

Elisha was thankful that the kind woman had helped him. She was quite old, and Elisha found out she had never been able to have a son. So what do you think he did? Elisha told her she *would* have a son, and God blessed her with one a year later! Helping others often brings unexpected rewards.

You can find this story in 2 Kings 4.

When You Pray, Day by Day
Ask God:
• to give you the desire to help meet the needs of elderly people in your neighborhood
• to help you have a happy heart when you do good things for others.
Thank God for loving everyone—including *you*.

Something Fun for Everyone
Fall leaves are fun to jump in, and they are pretty to collect and look at, too. But did you know many elderly and sick people seldom have a chance to enjoy the leaves? Here is a way you can take some of the beauty of fall to people who can't leave home.

Make long-lasting leaf bouquets. First, collect some of the most colorful fall leaves you can find. Next, lightly pound the base of stems and branches with a lightweight hammer (this will allow a preservative to be absorbed).

In a Jar or vase, combine these ingredients: one (1) part glycerin—which is available at many drug stores—and three (3) parts hot tap water. Stick the leaves and branches with crushed stems in a big vase or jar and use the leaves as a centerpiece in your home.

After the leaves are pliable—this will take from one to two weeks—remove them from the mixture. They will now feel much like crepe paper, and they will remain soft and pliable.

The last (and most important) step: Take bouquets of these pretty leaves to friends and neighbors whom you think may enjoy them. Add a friendly note with each bouquet.

Who's the Boss?
God's chain of authority

"I *won't* get my clothes on!" said Joy to her mother.

"Joy, I'm your mommy, and you need to do what I say."

Joy just stared at Mother. Finally, she began to get dressed. She didn't look happy.

57

Later that morning, Mrs. Bradley showed up with her three-year-old twin sons. Mother would be caring for them that day.

"No!" shouted Joy as Jacob Bradley started to climb onto the rocking horse. "That's my horse and I don't want you to ride it."

The rocking horse didn't really belong to Joy. It was a family toy that the children Mother watched were allowed to play with.

When Father came home from work that evening, he asked Joy to come talk to him.

"I hear you haven't had a very good day, honey," said Father as Joy climbed up on his lap. "Do you want to tell me about it?"

Joy made an unhappy face. "Everybody always bosses me," she said. "I don't like it."

"Honey, did you know everyone has a boss? We sometimes need someone to tell us what to do," said Father. "Mommy and I are your boss."

"I want to be my *own* boss," said Joy.

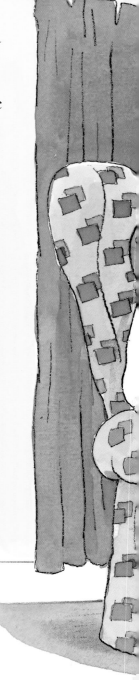

"God set things up so that others are our boss," said Father. "And that's good. It helps us have an orderly world."

"You and Mommy don't have a boss," said Joy.

"That's not true," answered Father. "I run our hardware store, but I still have a district manager who tells me what I should be doing."

59

"But Mommy doesn't have a boss," Joy argued.

"Not like I do," explained Father, "but Mommy and I both must do things that please God. You might say God is the Big Boss for all of us."

"Is God *my* boss too?" asked Joy.

"Yes, honey, He is. But He is a good and fair boss because He loves you so very much—just like Mommy and I do."

Joy thought about what Father had said. "If God wants me to have you and Mommy for a boss, I guess that's OK. But can't I be *someone's* boss?"

Father looked at the dolly in Joy's lap.

"Suzy needs to have someone tell her what food to eat so she won't get sick. And she'll need to be told when to come in out of bad weather. When Suzy has a cold, someone will have to take good care of her. Yes, Suzy needs a boss."

"Then I'll be Suzy's boss!" said Joy with a smile. "And I'll be a good boss to her because I love her."

Father gave Joy a kiss. "I'm sure you will, honey."

Check Your Head for What You've Read

1. Why didn't Joy want to get dressed when her mother told her to? Why did she tell Jacob Bradley he couldn't ride the rocking horse?
2. Why do people need to have a boss?
3. How do we know God will be a good and fair boss to us? How about your mother and father?

A Look Inside God's Special Book

When the world was new, God made Adam and Eve. They were in charge of the beautiful Garden of Eden. God told Adam and Eve they could eat of any tree in the garden except one—the tree of the knowledge of good and evil. He told them that if they ate of that tree's fruit, they would die.

One day Satan went to Eve. He was disguised as a snake. He said God had lied about the tree, and that eating its fruit wouldn't harm them. He told Eve the fruit would make them wise, that they would become like God. Eve thought she would like to be her own boss. So she ate some of the fruit. Adam ate some too.

God punished Adam and Eve and sent them away from the beautiful garden forever.

Read this story in Genesis 2–3.

When You Pray, Day by Day
Ask God:
• to show you why you need a boss
• to help you obey those in authority over you: your parents, pastor, teachers, and government officials.
Thank God that He has given you a good boss to love and care for you at home.

Something Fun for Everyone
Sometimes it helps to remind ourselves of the chain of authority God has set up for us.

Make a "Who's in Charge Here" chart.
The chart at the right shows God's chain of authority in the Kenton home. On a large sheet of heavy white paper, make a chart like this for *your* family. Write "Who's in Charge Here" in big letters across the top. Draw pictures of family members, your pastor, and school teachers (or use photographs). You might want to cut pictures of "Government Officials" (the President, your state's governor, policemen, and so on) out of magazines or newspapers. At the bottom of the page, write this week's Bible memory verse. Then hang the poster on your bedroom wall. Pray often for all those people who are above you on the chart. God has given each of them a very big job!

Bad Words Spell Trouble
Helping someone in need

"I'm at my wits' end," said Mrs. Smith. "I don't even know where Caleb *hears* such filthy language. We don't talk that way at our house. I just don't know what to do. . . ."

After Mrs. Smith had gone home, Father asked the children to gather around him and Mother.

"One of your friends is in trouble," said Father. "Mrs. Smith says Caleb has been using lots of bad language lately. His teacher kicked him out of class and won't let him return until she knows something is being done about the problem."

"It's bad all right," agreed Elaina. "We don't walk to school with him anymore. Everything Caleb sees is a blank-blank this or that. I hate it when he uses God's name as a bad word."

"Yes, it's wrong for him to say those things," said Mother. "We told Mrs. Smith we would try to help Caleb. Can you think of any ways we might do that?"

The children all thought for a minute.

"Why doesn't Mrs. Smith just spank Caleb?" suggested Joy.

"He's too big for that," answered Father. "The school counselor thinks Caleb is acting this way because his daddy doesn't live with the family anymore. He doesn't even live in this state. Spanking Caleb probably wouldn't help."

"Maybe I could spend more time with him," said Johnny. "I haven't been playing with him much because he's usually hanging around with other guys who like to swear."

"Your good influence might help," agreed Mother.

"What else can we do?"

"Dad?" said Johnny. "I know you're busy, but do you think *you* might be able to help Caleb?"

"What do you have in mind, Johnny?" asked Father.

"Well, I thought maybe you could spend a little time with him," Johnny answered. "You could talk with him about the bad language and about other problems that come up."

Let's Rehearse a Bible Verse

You must not use the name of the Lord your God
thoughtlessly. The Lord will punish anyone who is guilty
and misuses his name.

Exodus 20:7

"That might be a good idea, Johnny," said Father. "But it could mean I would have a little less time for you kids. What do you all think about my spending some time with Caleb?"

"It would be hard to have less time with you than I do now, Daddy," said Elaina. "But I think God might want me to share you a little bit."

"I think so too," agreed Joy, nodding her head of curls up and down.

Johnny nodded too, and Mother smiled.

"I'm proud of all of you," said Father. "It's good to put the needs of someone else ahead of your own. Why don't we pray that Jesus will show us how we can be the most help to Caleb?"

The family took each other's hands and bowed their heads while Father led them in prayer.

Check Your Head for What You've Read

1. Why did Caleb's teacher make him leave her classroom?
2. Why did the school counselor think Caleb had begun using bad words?
3. What were some ways the Kenton family thought they might be able to help Caleb?

A Look Inside God's Special Book

When people do bad things—such as say bad words—we usually don't want to be around them very much. But God isn't that way. Jesus once told a story about a shepherd who had one hundred sheep.

Jesus asked the people listening to Him what they thought the shepherd would do if he found out one night that one sheep was missing. Would the shepherd simply be happy he still had ninety-nine sheep? *NO*, Jesus said. He would search high and low until he found the missing sheep. *Then* he would be happy.

In the same way, Jesus said, God loves His people and rejoices when someone who has done something wrong turns to God.

Find this story in Luke 15 and Matthew 18.

When You Pray, Day by Day
Ask God:

• to help you avoid saying bad words, especially using God's name thoughtlessly

• to show you how to help people who have done wrong things turn to God.

Thank God that he loves you like the good shepherd loves his sheep.

Something Fun for Everyone

Because it's easy to forget how much God loves you, here's something that will remind you of His love.

Make a "Jesus Loves Me" cake. Follow the instructions that come with any sheet cake mix (the flavor doesn't matter), and pour the mixture into a 9-inch by 13-inch pan. When it's cool, frost the cake with white frosting.

Using the picture above as a guide, trace the outline of a lamb on the cake with a toothpick. Then decorate the lamb's body with coconut. (Color the coconut by placing it in a jar along with a few drops of food coloring, and shaking vigorously.) Decorate the eyes, nose, feet, and other features with raisins, nuts, chocolate chips, gumdrops, or cherry halves. After thanking God for loving each one of you, pour glasses of milk for everyone in your family, and enjoy your cake!

Note: You may also want to share your "Jesus Loves Me" cake with someone who *isn't* in your family, someone who you think might need to be reminded of God's love.

Some Time for a Friend
Knowing God's love—and parents' love

An occasional leaf dropped from tree branches and fell into the pond. Father and Caleb Smith sat together beside a tree. They watched their bobbers closely, hoping for a fish.

"How is school these days?" asked Father.

"A lot better, Mr. Kenton," said Caleb. "Thanks for asking Mrs. Kelleher to let me back into class. It wasn't any fun spending the whole day in the principal's office!

"I'm sorry I ever started using bad language. It's hard to stop doing it now. But I pray for help every morning before I go to school, just like you said I should. It's getting easier to use good words all the time."

"I'm glad to hear that, Caleb," said Father. "Is there anything else troubling you—anything you would like me to be praying about?"

A sad look crossed Caleb's face.

69

"Mr. Kenton," said Caleb, "I wish my family was like yours. My mommy and daddy were always arguing. Then Daddy went away. . . . Now I don't think Daddy loves me anymore." A tear slid down his cheek.

Father reached over and put a hand on Caleb's shoulder. "I'm sure he loves you, Caleb. God gave daddies a very strong love for their children."

"But I think *I* might be to blame for the divorce," said Caleb. "Sometimes I didn't mind Daddy like I should have. . . ."

"No, Caleb," Father answered. "You are not the reason your parents aren't together anymore. It's normal for you to feel this way, but it isn't true."

"If my daddy loves me, why didn't he stay married to my mom?" asked Caleb.

"Sometimes moms and dads stop loving each other, so they stop living together too," answered Father. "This makes God sad, but it happens anyway.

"But remember this, Caleb: Divorced parents may stop loving *each other*, but they *don't* stop loving their *children*.

"A parent's love doesn't depend on what happens in life. Even when our children *do* make mistakes, we go on loving them just like before."

Caleb wiped his eyes and cheeks with his hand and thought about what Father had said.

"My Sunday school teacher said God is like that," said Caleb. "Does God love us even when we do bad things?"

"Yes, Caleb," said Father. "The Bible says God loves us all, no matter what."

"But does He really love *me*?" Caleb asked.

70

"More than you can ever know. He only asks that you be His friend and love Him back."

"You're a good friend, Mr. Kenton. Maybe I should ask Jesus to be my friend too."

Father smiled. "Jesus will be happy to be your friend, Caleb. And you know something else?"

"What, Mr. Kenton?"

"Your bobber just went down!" said Father. "You've got a fish!"

71

Check Your Head for What You've Read

1. Why was Caleb afraid his daddy might not love him anymore? Do you think his daddy *really* stopped loving Caleb?
2. Do parents stop loving their children when their children do bad things or make mistakes?
3. How do you know Jesus wants to be your friend?

A Look Inside God's Special Book

Some of Jesus' best friends were fishermen. When Jesus was preaching one day, He asked Simon Peter, a fisherman, to take Him out on the lake. Jesus told Simon that if he put his nets into the water he would catch many fish. Simon didn't think that would happen. He had spent the whole night fishing and had caught nothing. But Simon obeyed Jesus anyway, and he caught so many fish that his nets began to break! Simon was amazed. He bowed down before Jesus.

"Don't be afraid," said Jesus to Simon and his friends. "From now on you will be fishermen for men." Simon became Jesus' friend that day.

Read more about this story in Luke 5.

When You Pray, Day by Day
Ask God:
• to help you know in your heart that your parents will never stop loving you
• to show you ways you can share Christ's love with others.
Thank God for loving you and wanting to be your friend, no matter what.

Something Fun for Everyone

Fish can be lots of fun. You may have fish in a bowl or tank in your home. And you may enjoy fishing for them in streams, ponds, or lakes.

Go "fishing for friends." Make a pond by covering a table with a sheet (or use a cardboard box). Cut some fish out of colored construction paper. Use markers for eyes and mouths, and glue and glitter to make the fish sparkle. Attach a metal paper clip to the head of each fish, then write the name of a friend or family member on each one.

Tie a long string to the end of a stick, and attach a magnet (such as the ones your mother may have on your refrigerator) to the end of the string. Put the fish in the pond and start fishing! After catching a fish, pray for the person the fish represents, thanking God for that person.

73

Thanks Anyway, God

Giving thanks when you don't feel thankful

The Kenton children were very excited as Mother and Father tucked them into bed. In the morning, they would be going to Grandma's house for Thanksgiving dinner.

While the children slept that night, the wind began to blow. Soon the rain started to pound against the windows. The whole house shook with the power of a mighty storm.

"Wow!" said Johnny when he looked out his bedroom window the next morning. The maple tree in the front yard now lay on its side across the driveway. There were tree branches and trash everywhere. He ran to tell his sisters.

Johnny found Joy and Elaina in their bedroom.

"Did you see what happened last night?" he began. "The big tree out front, it–Hey, what's wrong, Elaina?"

Elaina sniffed and wiped away a tear. "Mommy said we can't go to Grandma's now. The roads are blocked."

Johnny stood with his mouth open, shaking his head in disbelief. But Mother confirmed Elaina's sad report: The Kenton family would be staying home.

What a Thanksgiving this is going to be! thought Johnny. Just then Father came in from outside.

"Everything's a mess out there," he said. "A giant branch smashed through the roof of the Whites' house. I invited them to stay here with us until their roof is fixed. After cleaning up a little, they'll be here in time to eat Thanksgiving dinner with us."

"But the electricity isn't working anymore," said Joy. "How can Mommy fix Thanksgiving dinner?"

"Who cares," said Johnny in a gloomy voice. "We don't have anything to be thankful for anyway.

"Nothing to be thankful for?" said Mother. "Storms like this one often kill people. But we weren't even hurt! And as for dinner . . . well, we'll figure something out."

Johnny and Father went to the Whites' house to help them remove the tree branch. They covered the hole in the roof with thick black plastic.

When they arrived home with the Whites, Johnny saw candles burning. It was nearly dark outside, but the candles bathed the house in a warm, friendly glow.

Mother greeted them with a smile. "It isn't fancy, but it's dinner!" she said, pointing toward the table that had been set by the girls. "I used our camp stove to heat up some canned stew. And I managed to make some little biscuits, too."

"Isn't this lovely," said Virginia White.

"Yes," agreed Ralph. "It reminds me of some Thanksgivings I had as a boy."

The Kentons and Whites spent the entire dinner time talking about Thanksgiving memories.

"I think my favorite Thanksgiving memory may be the one I'm making today," said Ralph. Even in the dim lamplight, everyone could see he had tears of happiness in his eyes.

"I thank God for bringing such wonderful friends into our lives."

"And we thank God for both of you," said Father.

Mother and the children all smiled their agreement.

77

Check Your Head for What You've Read

1. Why didn't the Kentons get to go to Grandma's house for Thanksgiving?
2. Did the storm spoil the Kenton family's Thanksgiving dinner? Why not?
3. What did the Kentons have to be thankful for? How about Ralph and Virginia White?

A Look Inside God's Special Book

Have you ever been in a storm and been happy that God was there with you to protect you? One day Jesus and some of His followers got into a boat to cross a big lake.

Jesus fell asleep in the boat. As He slept, a big storm came up with strong wind and huge waves. The storm waves nearly sank the boat!

"We'll drown!" yelled the men in the boat. They woke Jesus and He immediately commanded the storm to stop.

The wind quit blowing and the lake became calm! Do you think the men were thankful that the Son of God was with them that day? We should be thankful that Jesus is with us, too.

You can read this story in Matthew 8; Mark 4; and Luke 8.

When You Pray, Day by Day
Ask God:

• to provide special Thanksgiving memories for you this year
• to show you how you can make this Thanksgiving special for someone else.
Thank God for His love, blessings, and protection now and throughout the year.

Something Fun for Everyone

It's easy to forget to give God the thanks He deserves for all the good things He does for us. That's why we need to find some ways to remind ourselves of God's goodness from time to time.

• **Play "Guess What I'm Thankful For" with your family.** The game works this way: One person at a time will give a clue, trying to help family members guess what he is thankful for. For example, if you are thankful for your church, you might say, "I am thankful for a group of people who teach me about God." If no one gives the right answer, give another clue. The person who guesses correctly then takes a turn trying to get others to guess what he or she is thankful for. (Make sure everyone gets a turn.)
• **Pray for a special family.** You might choose a different family to thank God for each night this week, or pray for the same family all week long. Form a circle and pray around the circle until someone has prayed for each member of the special family you are praying for that night.
• **Make Thanksgiving Cards.** For Thanksgiving day, make a "I'm thankful for you because . . ." card for each member of your family, and pass out the cards at dinner.

Fall–Week 13

Why Is Everything Ugly Now?

Appreciating God's creation

Joy and father were sitting in a lawn swing in their backyard. They were having a talk.

"Daddy, I just hate this time of year!" said Joy.

"Why is that, honey?" asked Father.

"Because there aren't many leaves on the trees, and the grass isn't pretty anymore," she answered. "And there aren't even any fireflies to catch and put in a jar."

"I'm sorry you're so unhappy, Joy," said Father. "But did you know we are surrounded by lots of beautiful things right now?"

"We are?" asked Joy.

"Sure," Father answered. "You just need to look at things a little *differently* right now. Let's go for a walk."

Father and Joy walked to a shady corner of the backyard. "What do you see in front of you, Joy?" he asked.

"Just the old birdbath," she answered. "And there aren't any birdies around anymore to play in the water."

"Most of the birds have flown south for the winter," said Father. "But look closely. Do you see anything else?"

Joy examined the birdbath carefully. "Oh, look at the pretty ice!" she said suddenly. "It looks like feathers!"

The afternoon was already cold and delicate ice crystals had begun to form in the water.

"Now look over there," said Father.

"It's just a big tree, Daddy," answered Joy. "It looks ugly without many leaves. Oh, wait!" she said suddenly. "Now I see something—a pretty gray squirrel!"

For several minutes they watched the squirrel hurry back and forth between a hazelnut tree and a hole at the base of a large maple tree.

"He's storing nuts for his winter food supply," said Father. "The maple tree is his home. Now look up."

81

Joy looked into the branches of a tree above her head. "Oh! The branches make pretty shapes!"

The bare branches of the tree crisscrossed this way and that, making shapes that looked to Joy like animals, flowers, and even castles.

"Now look up at the top of the tree," Father suggested.

"A bird's nest!" said Joy. "I didn't know there was a bird's nest in this tree."

"It's a robin's nest," said Father. "You couldn't see it when there were leaves on the tree."

"Daddy, it's fun to see all the beautiful things God has made," said Joy. "Are there pretty things to look at all year long?"

"You bet there are, honey," answered Father. "But sometimes we just need to know where to look. Soon there will be a blanket of snow on the ground, and icicles, and all the beauty of winter. But it will be cold!"

Joy had a thoughtful look on her face.

"That's OK, Daddy," she said finally. "God's world will be a good and special place then too. I'll just wear my coat and hat and mittens and go out to look at all the pretty things of winter!"

Father put his hand on his daughter's head, and smiled.

Let's Rehearse a Bible Verse

God looked at everything he had made, and it was very good.

Genesis 1:31

Check Your Head for What You've Read

1. Why was Joy unhappy at first?

2. What did Father mean when he told Joy we sometimes need to look at things in a different way in order to see the beauty of God's creation?

3. What things did Father show Joy that helped her appreciate God's world more?

A Look Inside God's Special Book

Do you ever think about God's creation? God made the earth and sky and moon and stars from nothing! He made the wind and rain, the sun and moon. He made the oceans and lakes and rivers and streams—and filled them with fish. And God made the grass and plants and trees.

God also made animals of every imaginable kind: rabbits and bears, turtles and lions, giraffes and bumble bees. He made ostriches with fluffy tail feathers. And He made graceful doves and busy hummingbirds. Then God made people to take care of and enjoy the things He had created. And He did all this—and much more—in just six days!

Read more about the creation story in Genesis 1–2.

When You Pray, Day by Day
Ask God:
• to help you always be able to see that all of God's creation is good
• to show you how to help others appreciate the special things about each season of the year.
Thank God for making such a beautiful, wonderful world for us to live in.

Something Fun for Everyone
It's good to take a close look sometimes at God's creation. Do you ever wonder how ice forms when the weather gets cold? Or how any kind of crystals grow, for that matter? Let's watch it happen!

Grow a salt crystal landscape. You will need to work with your parents on this to ensure safety. Take an aluminum pie pan or a shallow glass dish, and pile up a stack of absorbent materials in it—things like tree bark, cork, Styrofoam, sponge, or porous rock.

Then mix a salt solution. Start with four tablespoons of water in a pint jar or small pitcher. Mix in four tablespoons of noniodized table salt, four tablespoons of liquid bluing, and one tablespoon of ammonia. Dribble this solution over the objects in your pan or dish. (Make sure the salt solution covers the bottom of the container.) You may drip food coloring over your landscape for an even more interesting effect!

Put your landscape where it won't have to be moved, and watch what happens this week as the water evaporates, leaving crystals behind. God's world is truly amazing!

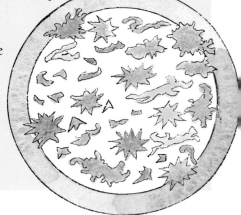

WINTER

December
January
February

Christmas (Week 1, 2, & 3)
New Year's (Week 4)
Valentine's Day (Week 10)

I Don't Think I Can Do It!
Trusting Christ for courage

"Mommy! Daddy!" Elaina said as she came in the front door. "I'm going to sing a solo in the Sunday school Christmas program!"

"That's wonderful, honey!" said Mother.

"You have a beautiful singing voice, Elaina," said Father. "I know you'll do just fine."

Elaina smiled and looked a little embarrassed.

"Do you really think so, Daddy?" she asked. "I'm a little scared."

"Just do your best and have fun," he answered.

Each Sunday school class was going to sing a Christmas song or do a skit. Elaina's first grade class was going to sing "Away in a Manger," with Elaina singing the first verse and the whole class singing the others.

Elaina practiced hard all week.

"Can we practice one more time before we go to the church, Mommy?" asked Elaina. It was Saturday, the day of the Christmas program rehearsal.

"Yes," said Mother. "But you already know the song very well. I don't think you need to worry."

86

Mother played the piano as Elaina sang through the song three more times.

That afternoon, as Mother was about to leave with her children for the church, she looked all around.

"Joy, where's your sister?" she asked.

"She told me she was going to stay home with Daddy," Joy answered in a matter-of-fact voice.

Mother went to the girls' room, where she found Elaina sitting on her bed. She gave her mother a stubborn look.

"I've decided not to go," she said.

"But why, sweetie?" asked Mother.

"Because I'm afraid!" Elaina answered. "I just don't think I can stand up in front of a bunch of people and sing." She began to cry.

"I want to tell you a secret," said Mother. "When I was your age I was *terribly* shy about getting up in front of groups."

"Really, Mommy?" said Elaina. "You do things like that all the time now."

"That's because I learned something important," she answered. "My grandmother reminded me that Jesus was *always* with me. So I started trusting Him to help me remember words to songs, my lines in plays, and things like that. I was still nervous, but knowing that Jesus was with me helped me be brave."

"I don't think I can ever be as brave as you, Mommy," said Elaina.

"Sure you can, honey," she answered. "Just ask Jesus to help. He'll be right there with you."

"I've never done this before," Elaina said. "I think I'll need to be especially brave today. Are you sure Jesus will help me?"

"I know He will," Mother answered. "Let's bow our heads right now and pray that He'll help you be extra brave today."

Let's Rehearse a Bible Verse

Remember that I commanded you to be strong and brave. So don't be afraid. The Lord your God will be with you everywhere you go.

Joshua 1:9

Check Your Head for What You've Read

1. Why did Elaina decide she didn't want to be in the Sunday school Christmas program?

2. Who helped Elaina's mother overcome her own fear of getting up in front of groups?

3. What did Elaina's mother learn from her grandmother that helped her to be brave?

A Look Inside God's Special Book

One night some of Jesus' followers began to cross a large lake in a boat. Jesus stayed behind to pray. The wind came up, and the boat was tossed about on the waves. Jesus saw that His friends were in trouble. So He walked to them on the water!

His friends saw Jesus coming and were afraid. They thought they were seeing a ghost. But Jesus told them who He was and asked them to be brave. Peter tried to walk across the water to Jesus. Suddenly he became afraid and looked at the wind and the waves. When he took his eyes off Jesus, Peter lost his courage and sank into the water. Jesus rescued him and calmed the wind.

You can find this story in Matthew 14 and Mark 6.

When You Pray, Day by Day
Ask God:

• to help you be brave when you have to do something that is difficult for you

• to show you how you can learn to trust Him more.

Thank God for always being near so that He can help when you when you need courage.

Something Fun for Everyone

Having the courage to speak or perform before a group is something everyone needs to work at. The following ideas can help.

• Practice singing a song, reading, or reciting a poem.
Then ask your family to gather around to hear it. Next, go to a friend's house and do the same thing for your friend's family.

• Use a tape recorder as a confidence booster. Record songs you will perform or lines you will be doing in plays. You may be surprised at how your voice sounds on tape, but hearing yourself perform well can boost your confidence. And a recording can show you areas where you still need more practice.

• Secret Weapon Number 1: Pray, pray, pray! Jesus really does want to help. Ask Him.

Reminder: If you make mistakes when you're in front of a group, *that's OK*. It happens to everyone. People will not like you any less—and that's a promise!

A Special Visit
Using your talents for God

It was Sunday, just a few days before Christmas. The Sunday school Christmas program would be that night.

Mother was talking on the phone. "Will the five o'clock bus be on time?" she asked. "Thank you!" She hung up the phone.

"Is someone coming for a visit?" asked Johnny.

Mother smiled. "I guess I can tell you now. Grandma is coming for Christmas!"

"Grandma's coming! Grandma's coming!" yelled Joy. She and Elaina joined hands and started jumping up and down, bouncing around the room.

Mother and the children arrived at the church at 5:30. The program would begin at six.

"Will Daddy and Grandma get here in time to hear me sing?" asked Elaina.

"They should," answered Mother. "I told your father I would save them a place to sit."

Mother took a seat in the front row. Elaina, Joy, and Johnny sat down with their Sunday school classes.

Elaina smiled as the first group, the beginners, went up on the stage. They were wearing costumes, and Joy was dressed like a fuzzy sheep! Their teacher read from the Bible, then the beginners sat down again.

When the kindergarten class went up on stage, Elaina realized her class was next. She started to feel nervous, but suddenly she remembered that Jesus would be there with her. She felt calm and confident again.

Once on stage, Elaina checked to see if Grandma and Father had arrived. The two seats by Mother were still empty. The lady at the piano began to play, and Elaina opened her mouth to sing . . . but nothing came out.

93

The piano player just smiled and started over. This time Elaina came in when she was supposed to. Her voice was loud and clear. Elaina sang the first verse of "Away in a Manger," then her class joined with her to sing the others.

Elaina was worried as she watched the rest of the program. *Is Grandma all right?* she wondered.

Pastor Halperin ended the program by inviting everyone to stay for cookies and punch.

Once in the fellowship hall, Elaina looked for her family. She spotted Mother, Joy, and Johnny on the other side of the room. Behind them she saw Father . . . and *Grandma!* She ran across the room.

"What happened, Grandma?" she asked after a long hug. "Why were you late?"

"The bus had a flat tire, honey," she said.

Elaina glanced down at the floor. "I had a solo tonight, Grandma. I'm sorry you didn't hear it."

"But I did!" she answered. "Your daddy and I arrived just in time. You sounded like an angel."

"You really liked it?"

"It was beautiful. It makes me very happy when my grandchildren use their talents for God. Your Grandpa would have been *so* proud. . . ."

Grandma had a tear in her eye. But suddenly she smiled. "I'm hungry. Would anyone like to come with me to get cookies and punch?"

She had three eager volunteers.

Let's Rehearse a Bible Verse

We all have different gifts.
Each gift came because of the grace that
God gave us.

Romans 12:6

95

Check Your Head for What You've Read

1. Who was the Kentons' special Christmas visitor?
2. Why was the children's grandmother late for the Christmas program?
3. Why was Grandma happy that Elaina had sung a solo? Do you think it's important to use our talents for God?

A Look Inside God's Special Book

God gives each of us particular gifts and talents. King Solomon was given the gift of wisdom. In fact, he was the wisest man on earth. One day, two women came to Solomon with a baby. Both of them claimed to be the baby's mother.

Because Solomon didn't know which woman was the real mother, he thought up a test. "Cut the baby in two," he commanded, "and give half of it to each woman." The real mother would have none of that! She said no, but the other woman said yes. Solomon now knew who the real mother was. He gave the baby to the woman who didn't want the baby killed. Solomon had used his gift of wisdom well!

Read more about Solomon in 1 Kings 1–8.

When You Pray, Day by Day

Ask God:

• to help you learn how to recognize and use your gifts and talents to their full potential

• to show you ways your talents can be used to tell others about God's love.

Thank God for giving you abilities that make you special and different from everyone else.

Something Fun for Everyone

Everywhere we turn this time of year we see reminders of Christ's birth and God's grace. But many people don't know much about the true meaning of Christmas. Why not use your God-given talents to share the Good News of Jesus this Christmas? The following are some ways to do that.

• **Make a Christmas card.** Draw a picture of Jesus in a manger, and write inside the card some reasons Christmas is special to you. Include a Bible verse (John 3:16 is a good one).

• **Read the Christmas story.** Read aloud for your friends from your Bible or Bible storybook. (The Christmas story is in Matthew 1–2 and Luke 2.)

• **Write a letter.** This is a good way to tell someone what Jesus means to you. A parent or other adult can help you do this.

• **Sing.** Many songs can help others know more about Jesus' love. Elderly people in particular appreciate music.

• **Perform a Christmas play or skit.** Do this with or without other performers. You may want to use puppets. (See the activity for Fall–WEEK 3 for some puppet-making ideas.)

Note: Don't worry about doing a perfect job when you share God's Good News—_He_ will make the message meaningful to the people who hear it.

God's Gift of Life
Praying for God's intervention

It was Christmas Eve. Father had just finished reading the Christmas story in the Bible, and it was time for the children to go to bed.

"Mommy, you might as well let us stay up, because we're too excited to sleep," said Elaina.

"You can say that again!" agreed Johnny.

"Nice try, kids," said Mother. "Come on now, off to bed—tomorrow will be a very big day!"

Just then Joy grabbed her throat with both hands. She made a strange sound but couldn't talk. She was having trouble breathing.

"I think she's choking!" screamed Grandma. "Help her!"

Father grabbed Joy and gave her a sharp swat on the back to try to loosen what was caught in her windpipe. It did no good.

"Call for help!" he yelled.

Within a few minutes an ambulance arrived. Joy's skin had begun to turn blue. The medics rushed Joy out of the house to the ambulance, which took her to the hospital. Mother and Father went with her.

Grandma, Johnny, and Elaina listened until the ambulance's

siren could no longer be heard in the distance. They all had red eyes from crying.

"Could Joy die, Grandma?" asked Johnny.

"Let's pray that God will protect her," Grandma answered as she sat down in Mother's rocking chair. The three of them joined hands, making a circle. Then they bowed their heads.

"Dear Lord," Grandma began, "save little Joy's life. We love her so much. Please make her well. I ask this of You in Jesus' name."

Johnny and Elaina prayed for their sister too. Then Grandma prayed some more.

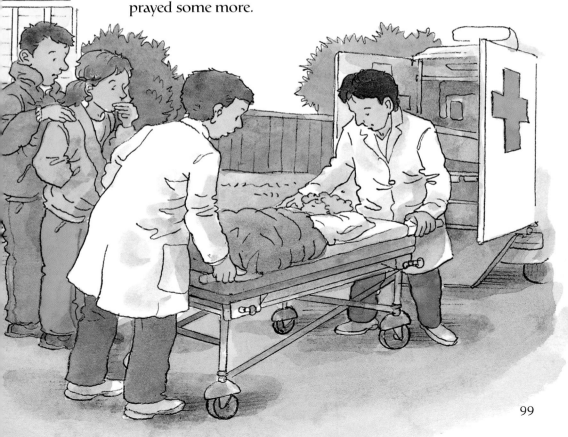

"No matter what happens, Lord," Grandma said as she brought the prayer to an end, "we will love and honor You. We know You always do what's right."

After the prayer, Grandma and her grandchildren continued to hold hands for a long time. Grandma jumped up when the phone rang.

Let's Rehearse a Bible Verse

Today your Savior was born in David's town.
He is Christ, the Lord.

Luke 2:11

"Kenton residence," she answered quickly. A moment later she said, "Oh, that's wonderful news!" She turned to Elaina and Johnny. "Joy is going to be OK!"

"Yes! Thank You, God!" said Johnny as he began jumping up and down. Elaina joined him. Tears of happiness streamed down their cheeks.

After an hour or so, Mother and Father came home. Joy was asleep in Father's arms.

"A sharp piece of candy cane was wedged in her windpipe," explained Father. "When we got to the hospital, Joy stopped breathing entirely.

"She was in great danger, but . . ." Father's eyes filled with tears. "But we could feel God's power in the room. The candy suddenly came loose and popped out into the doctor's hand."

"What a wonderful Christmas!" said Mother. "Not only will we celebrate God's gift of His Son, but we'll thank Him for another special gift–the gift of Joy's life."

Check Your Head for What You've Read

1. Why did Joy have to go to the hospital?

2. What did the children's grandmother do with Elaina and Johnny after Joy went to the hospital?

3. Can you name at least two things the Kentons have to celebrate about this Christmas?

A Look Inside God's Special Book

When Jesus was born, most people who heard the news were happy. But not everyone. When King Herod in Jerusalem heard, he wanted to kill Jesus. He was afraid Jesus would try to take away his kingdom someday.

Three wise men who had come from countries far away went to Herod to ask where they could find Jesus. They wanted to worship Him. Herod didn't know where Jesus was, but he asked the wise men to come back and tell him when they found Him. In a dream, God told the wise men not to tell King Herod where Jesus was. How different things would be for us today if Jesus had been killed when He was a baby!

Find this story in Matthew 2.

When You Pray, Day by Day
Ask God:
• to help you appreciate His sacrifice in sending Jesus to us to die for our sins
• to protect you and each of your family members from harm.
Thank God for His gifts to you of Jesus, life, and love.

Something Fun for Everyone
At this busy time of year, we sometimes forget how precious our family is to us. Why not have a quiet family appreciation night this week? Here are some things you can do.

• **Rent and watch a Christmas video or DVD.** *It's a Wonderful Life* is a good choice. It shows us that the life God has given us is worth living no matter what our problems.
• **Look at family photo albums, videos, DVDs, and scrapbooks**. You'll remember fun things you have done as a family for the rest of your life.
• **Make a simple snack plate.** Cut up some fresh fruit and vegetables (red and green ones would be fun this time of year!) and buy some dips. Add crackers, cheese, popcorn—whatever you like!
• **Mix up your favorite punch.** If you don't have a favorite, follow this simple recipe: In a punch bowl combine a 6-ounce can of frozen juice with a one-liter bottle of club soda. Top the punch with colorful scoops of sherbet.
Remember: The object of this special evening is to appreciate your family, so let them know you love them. And have lots of fun!

A New Year's Revolution

Obeying parents

The Kenton family planned to have a lazy day to celebrate the first day of the year. Everyone slept late, because they had attended a New Year's Eve party at the church the night before.

"I have an idea," announced Father after everyone was finally up. "It's too late for breakfast and too early for lunch. So let's go to a restaurant and have *brunch*."

"That sounds like fun," said Mother.

The children agreed.

After arriving at the restaurant, the Kenton children seemed unusually loud and rowdy.

"Please be on your best behavior today, kids," said Father. "A restaurant is a public place, and it's important to be thoughtful of others."

But the children seemed to quickly forget what Father had said.

"They don't have anything good on the menu," Johnny complained. "Do you remember what happened the last time we were here? They put onions on my hamburger and wrecked it. And I didn't get enough french fries, either."

"Oh yuck, *onions*," said Elaina. "They're *so* icky!"

"The food here is just fine," said Mother.

Just then Joy climbed down from her chair and started crawling around under the table. Father picked her up off the floor and set her back down firmly. A lady at a nearby table frowned.

The waitress wrote the Kentons' order and soon returned with their drinks. She explained that it would be a few more minutes before their food was ready.

"They sure are *slow* here," said Johnny as the waitress started to walk away.

Father was about to talk to Johnny about the rude thing he had said, when he heard a woman say, "Oh, my!" Father and Mother turned to see what had happened.

They saw Elaina with a straw in her mouth. She had blown the straw's wrapper across the room, where it hit a woman in the face. Mother saw that the woman was the mother of one of the children she sometimes took care of during the day.

Mother took Elaina by the hand and led her over to the woman so that Elaina could apologize.

On the way home, the car was quiet. The children knew their behavior hadn't been good.

"We didn't start the new year off very well, did we, kids?" said Father.

No one answered.

"Elaina, did you know I have been sharing about Jesus with the lady you hit with a straw wrapper?" asked Mother. "What do you suppose she thinks about Christians now?"

"I'm sorry, Mommy," Elaina answered quietly.

"Kids, the Bible tells us to be considerate of others," said Father. "It also says we should be careful of what we do because our actions can turn people against Jesus."

"I wish we could start this day over," said Johnny.

"We can't do that," said Father. "But you *can* all promise to be more considerate of others. And you can ask Jesus to help you keep your promise."

Johnny, Joy, and Elaina all nodded their heads in agreement.

Check Your Head for What You've Read

1. Did the Kenton children obey their father at the restaurant? What did they do that was wrong?

2. Do you think their poor behavior could have made people think bad things about Jesus?

3. What did Father ask the children to promise? Who could help them keep this promise?

A Look Inside God's Special Book

Sometimes we can't see the reason behind what we are told to do. A visitor to Israel named Naaman felt that way. Naaman had a skin disease called leprosy. Through a messenger, the prophet Elisha told him to wash himself in the Jordan River seven times. Elisha had said this would cure his leprosy.

Naaman was angry. He thought Elisha's God should heal him instantly. And he thought the rivers in his homeland were better than the Jordan River anyway. Naaman didn't obey, and the leprosy wouldn't go away. Finally, Naaman decided to do what Elisha told him to, even though he thought it was foolish. He obeyed and was healed!

Read this story in 2 Kings 5.

When You Pray, Day by Day
Ask God:
• to help you this year to be more thoughtful of people in public places and at home
• to help you obey your parents, pleasing both them and the Lord.
Thank God for His desire to forgive you and to love you when you do something wrong.

Something Fun for Everyone
People aren't born knowing how to act in public places—it's something we all must learn. And as you probably know by now—learning can be fun!

Below is a family game that can help you practice good manners for public places.

Play restaurant in your home. Here's what you do: You be the waiter or waitress in your restaurant. Your brothers or sisters can be other restaurant workers (such as a hostess or a person who clears tables). Your parents are customers.

Study how your parents act as you take their order. Are they noisy and rude? Do they fight with each other or climb around under the table? Probably not. Are they considerate of other customers? Probably so.

Now switch places with your parents. You're the *customer* now. Copy your parents' good restaurant behavior. Be courteous with workers when you don't like what is on the menu, and be patient when it takes them a long time to bring your food. What other good things did your parents do?

Note: If it's OK with your parents, serve each other breakfast when you play restaurant!

Winter—Week 5

A Winter Adventure
Trusting God for protection

Johnny and Champion were especially happy today as they hiked along a dirt road through the woods. The weather had been very cold, and they were headed for their favorite ice-skating pond.

"Wow, look how thick the ice is!" said Champion when they reached the pond.

"Yeah, Dad checked it out yesterday," replied Johnny.

"He says it's nearly a foot thick."

The boys sat on a log at the edge of the pond and put on their skates. It was a gray day.

"The sky's getting darker," Johnny said. "It looks like it might snow."

"I hope so," said Champion. "I got a new sled for Christmas and haven't used it yet."

For the next hour the boys skated as hard as they ever had. They loved the feel of the cold air against their faces as they raced across the ice.

"Look!" said Champion. "It's starting to snow!"

A few tiny snowflakes now were falling and blowing around in little swirls on the ice.

"The wind is coming up too," said Johnny. "Maybe we should leave."

"No way!" said Champion. "I'm not ready to go yet. Who's afraid of a few snowflakes?"

Johnny reluctantly agreed to stay for another half hour. It would begin to get dark soon after that, he knew, and he had to be home before dark.

As they played, the boys suddenly heard a sharp *snap!* They turned around in time to see a pine bough break loose from a tree. The wind had come up quickly, and now the trees were wildly swaying and bending.

Along with the wind came heavy snow. The boys suddenly were frightened. They could barely see as the wind drove a

110

thick cloud of stinging snow into their faces.

"Let's go over there," said Johnny, pointing toward an old shack left from when a logging company was here years earlier. "Maybe we can wait inside until the wind and snow let up."

The boys found the shack unlocked, and they hurried inside. It was empty except for some old cardboard boxes and a worn-out tarp.

The wind howled outside and blew snow in under the door and through a broken pane in the shack's only window. The boys fastened a piece of cardboard over the window, and

111

wedged another piece under the door. It was now quite dark inside.

"I'm getting scared," said Champion. "We could freeze in here!"

The boys sat down together on some flattened cardboard boxes and wrapped up in the tarp.

"I'm scared too," said Johnny. "But I believe God will protect us."

"What makes you think so?" asked Champion. "People freeze to death all the time."

"God loves us and takes care of His people," answered Johnny. "Let's pray for His protection."

"Uh . . . OK . . . sure, Johnny," said Champion. "I guess we don't have a choice but to trust in God."

With the old shack shaking from the power of the violent storm, Johnny led the boys in prayer.

> ## Let's Rehearse a Bible Verse
>
> The Lord is your protection.
> You have made God Most High your place of safety.
>
> Psalm 91:9

Check Your Head for What You've Read

1. Why did Johnny and Champion suddenly decide to seek shelter in the old logging shack?
2. What did the boys do to protect themselves from the cold and snow?
3. In what ways had God protected the boys even before Johnny prayed?

A Look Inside God's Special Book

God often protects and provides for His people in surprising ways. The prophet Elijah told King Ahab that God was going to punish him for the wrong things he had done. Ahab wanted to kill Elijah. So God sent Elijah away.

God punished King Ahab with a drought–a long time when no rain would fall. But with no rain, Elijah wouldn't have water to drink. And he had no food. So God led him to a hidden stream where he could get water. And God had ravens carry food to Elijah twice a day! In this way God protected Elijah from the king and from the fearsome heat and dry weather.

Find this story in 1 Kings 17.

When You Pray, Day by Day
Ask God:
• to help you know when you are in danger and to help you to find safety
• to protect you from harm, both from dangers you see and from those hidden from you.
Thank God for His love, protection, and provision in times of need.

Something Fun for Everyone
Winter is a time of great beauty. But the cold and storms of winter can be dangerous. It's a time to be very careful!

Make a winter safety chart. On a large sheet of white construction paper or poster board, write out the following safety checklist. Add to the list any additional guidelines your parents would like you to remember. Look at the list before you go out to play, and check off each item in your head. Then go have fun!

❒ Do I have my parents' or sitter's permission to go outside? Do they know *exactly* where I will be?

❒ Am I dressed warmly enough? Do I have my hat, coat, gloves or mittens, and scarf? Do I need boots? If I am going out into the woods, do I have emergency food?

❒ If I am going away from the house or apartment, will a friend be with me at all times in case there is an accident?

❒ If I am going ice skating or sledding, have my parents made sure the ice or sledding site is safe? (It is almost *always* necessary to have an adult with you when you are ice skating on a pond or lake.)

❒ Do I know what the weather is supposed to be like today? Will I have shelter if there is unexpected snow?

❒ When do my parents expect me back home? Do I have a watch with me to keep track of time?

❒ Have I prayed for God's protection today?

A Night to Remember
Answered prayer: A time for thanks

Johnny and Champion huddled together under an old tarp as a blizzard raged outside.

"B-r-r-r-r! It's *so* cold! Do you think anyone will find us out here?" Champion asked.

"Of course they will," answered Johnny. "Our parents know where we went skating."

"Yeah, I know. But will they find us *before* we become Popsicles?"

Johnny normally would have laughed at Champion's joke. But he didn't this time. He was too cold—and too frightened.

"I . . . I just wonder what's keeping them," said Johnny. "They should have been here by now."

Johnny got up from underneath the tarp and felt his way along the floor to the door. It had been dark outside for several hours. He put his ear to the door to see if he could hear anyone or anything.

The only sounds he heard were those of the storm. He heard the eerie, high-pitched whistle of the wind as it curled around the corners of the building, and he could hear tree branches rubbing roughly against the roof.

Johnny curled up under the tarp again. "The Lord is my shepherd. I have everything I need," he recited. "He gives me rest in green pastures. He leads me to calm water. He gives me new strength. . . . Even if I walk through a very dark valley, I will not be afraid because you are with me."

"What's that you're saying?" asked Champion.

"It's from the Bible," answered Johnny. "It's called the Twenty-third Psalm. My grandfather once told me that nothing is more comforting in times of danger than Scripture."

"Do you know any more?" asked Champion.

"I sure do," answered Johnny. He began to recite as many Bible verses and passages as he could remember. Soon they both drifted off to sleep.

The boys awoke to a pounding sound. Someone was knocking at the door of the shack with a shovel handle. Then they heard a voice. . . .

"Hello! Is anyone in there?"

117

It was Father!

"Yes, Dad! We're here!" shouted Johnny. The boys heard the clanging sound of shovels. Then the door burst open.

Let's Rehearse a Bible Verse

When I am afraid, I will trust you.

Psalm 56:3

"Johnny!" said Father. "Are you boys all right?"

"Dad!" said Champion as his own father followed Mr. Kenton through the door.

After hugs had been exchanged all around, the boys went with their fathers out into the cold sunshine to the waiting four-wheel-drive truck.

The boys were amazed to see that some two feet of snow had fallen overnight, with snowdrifts deeper than the boys were tall!

Once they were inside the truck, all wrapped up in blankets and drinking hot chocolate, Father said, "I think we owe Someone a big thank you."

Then he bowed his head and thanked God for protecting the boys in the biggest snowstorm to hit the area in many years.

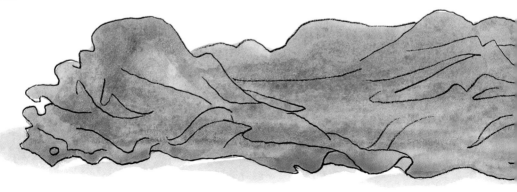

Check Your Head for What You've Read

1. What was Johnny hoping to hear when he listened in the dark at the door of the shack?

2. Why do you think it took the boys' fathers so long to find them?

3. What did Johnny do that made both boys feel safer as the storm raged outside?

A Look Inside God's Special Book

Sometimes we need to be patient when we're waiting for God to deliver us from danger. Noah and his family were tossed around in the ark by a fierce rain storm that lasted several weeks. Finally, the rain stopped falling. But Noah's ordeal wasn't over. The *whole world* was covered with water!

Noah sent a dove out to look for land. But there was no dry land yet, so the dove came back. Later, Noah sent the dove out again. This time the bird brought back an olive branch. The third time Noah sent out a dove, it didn't come back. It had found a home on dry land. When the ark came to rest on the land again, Noah thanked God for keeping his family safe.

Read more about Noah in Genesis 6–9.

119

When You Pray, Day by Day

Ask God:

• to help you remember Him and His love during times of danger

• to help you memorize Scripture so that you will be comforted by God's Word when you are in need.

Thank God for all the times He has protected you and kept you from harm.

Something Fun for Everyone

God's Scriptures can be a great comfort to you when you are lonely or afraid. The following fun ideas can help you learn some Bible verses.

• **Make Bible flashcards.** Write the following Scripture verses on colored 3-inch by 5-inch note cards (only one verse per card). On the unlined side of the card write the *Bible reference only*. With the reference side up, quiz yourself, trying to remember the verse on the other side of the card. Even better, have someone play with you, and quiz each other!

• 2 Timothy 4:7–8 • John 3:16 • Romans 8:32 • John 15:13 • 2 Corinthians 9:8 • Romans 8:28 • 1 John 15:9 • 1 John 5:4–5

• **Make Bible-verse puzzles.** Draw some large shapes or objects on a sheet of poster board (animals and fish work well). Cut them out. Write a Scripture verse or passage on each shape. Then cut each shape into puzzle pieces. (*Hint*: Unless your puzzles are different colors, keep the puzzle pieces in separate envelopes.)

Note: Your parents or Sunday school teacher may know some other good Bible memory games.

There's Nothing to Do!
Finding joy in helping others

"Mommy, I'm bored," said Elaina.

"Why's that, honey?" asked Mother.

"It's too cold and windy to go outside and play," she answered. "And I can't think of anything else to do."

Mother looked thoughtful for a minute.

"Here's an idea, Elaina," said Mother. "One of the best ways to keep from being bored is to do something special for someone else. Why don't we bake cookies for someone today?"

121

"That's a good idea, Mommy!" answered Elaina. "When can we start?"

"You, Joy, and I have the whole afternoon to ourselves," said Mother. "Let's start right now!"

After they all put on aprons, Mother got together the cookie ingredients.

The girls stood on chairs at the counter and watched as Mother broke an egg into a big mixing bowl. She added sugar and other things, then the girls took turns stirring the mixture.

Next, the girls sifted in flour and the remaining ingredients. Mother laughed as a cloud of flour dust rose around Elaina and Joy. Even their eyebrows turned white! After they finished making the dough, Mother showed the girls how to roll it into little balls. They dipped the dough balls in sugar and put them in neat rows on a cookie sheet.

"They smell yummy," said Joy as the cookies baked. Through the oven window, they watched the balls of dough flatten out on the cookie sheet.

Soon they had baked a big pile of warm cookies. Mother put some of them into a plastic container, then wrapped the container in kitchen towels and placed it into a basket.

Wearing their heavy coats, hats, and mittens, Mother and the girls set off down the street.

"Welcome, friends!" said Ralph White as he answered the knock at his door. "Come in before you catch your death of cold!"

"What a wonderful surprise!" said

Virginia White as she spread the cookies out on a plate. "Don't they look delicious!"

"They don't just *look* good," said Mr. White with a smile as he bit into a cookie.

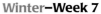

123

"We helped Mommy make them," said Elaina proudly.

Ralph delighted the girls with stories about his and Virginia's career as missionaries in Mexico. Before they knew it, they had visited with the Whites for more than an hour.

"It's time to go now, girls," said Mother as she got up and put on her coat.

"So soon?" asked Elaina.

"I'm afraid so, honey," answered Mother. "It will be getting dark soon."

"Thanks for the cookies. And God bless you all," said Ralph White as Mother and the girls left.

"This has been a really fun day," said Elaina as they carefully made their way along the icy street.

"We got to eat lots of cookies, too!" added Joy.

"When we do nice things for other people, it not only makes *them* happy, it makes *Jesus* happy," said Mother.

"And that's not all," said Elaina. "It makes *us* happy too. Isn't that right, Mommy?"

Mother smiled. "Yes, honey," she said. "It makes us happy too."

> ### Let's Rehearse a Bible Verse
>
> Be kind and loving to each other.
>
> Ephesians 4:32

Check Your Head for What You've Read

1. What did Mother suggest Elaina do so she wouldn't be bored anymore?
2. How did Joy and Elaina help their mother with their cookie-baking project?
3. When we do good things for other people, we make them happy. Who else is made happy?

A Look Inside God's Special Book

One day some of Jesus' friends had a dinner for Him. Martha fixed the food. But Mary did something that surprised everyone: she poured expensive perfume on Jesus' feet, then wiped His feet with her long hair.

Judas Iscariot, the disciple who would later betray Jesus, complained about what Mary had done. He said she should have sold the perfume and given the money to the poor. But Jesus said Mary was right to have done this special thing for Him, because He wouldn't be with them much longer.

If we wait to do nice things for people, we may never get the chance to do them!

Find this story in John 12.

When You Pray, Day by Day
Ask God:
• to help you be alert for ways you can do special things for people–especially elderly people
• to help you want to do acts of kindness today, because tomorrow may be too late.

Thank God for making you happy when you do nice things for others.

Something Fun for Everyone
Home-baked items–such as cookies–make great gifts. And they can be quite easy to make (with the help of an adult!). Why not give the following recipe a try?

Bake a batch of ginger snaps!
Following the recipe below, make some cookies to share. These cookies look great and taste even better!

Ingredients

3/4	*cup shortening*
1	*cup sugar*
1/4	*cup molasses*
1	*egg*
2	*teaspoons baking soda*
2	*cups sifted all-purpose flour*
1/2	*teaspoon cloves*
1/2	*teaspoon ginger*
1/2	*teaspoon salt*

Melt the shortening over low heat in a 3- or 4-quart saucepan. Remove the pan from the heat. Let it cool. Then add the sugar, molasses, and egg. Beat the mixture well. Sift together the flour, baking soda, salt, and spices. Add this to the first mixture. Mix it well and chill in the refrigerator.

Form the dough into one-inch diameter balls. Roll the balls in granulated sugar and place them two inches apart on a greased cookie sheet. Bake the cookies in a moderately hot oven (375° F) for eight to ten minutes. Remove them from the oven and let them cool. They're ready to eat!

Note: The elderly and shut-ins will appreciate your visit even more than your cookies! So plan to stay for a few minutes to talk with them.

A Sad Day, a Glad Day
Dealing with death

"Kenton residence," said Father as he answered the phone.
  "I'm sorry to bother you, Steve, but I'm worried about Ralph." It was Virginia White on the phone.
  "What's wrong?" asked Father.

127

"Well, he's having trouble breathing, and he says he has sharp pains in his chest and arm," she answered.

"I'll be right there," said Father.

At the Whites' house, Father found Ralph White sitting hunched over at the kitchen table.

"I . . . I'll be fine . . . in a few minutes," Ralph said. "It must . . . I think it was something . . . I ate. . . ."

"Let's go to the hospital and get this checked out, Ralph," said Father.

Father and Virginia helped him to the car.

"He's had a serious heart attack," said the doctor at the hospital. "I'm not sure he'll make it through the day."

Mrs. White began to cry. Father put his strong arm around her shoulder and comforted her.

"He's been asking for you," said the doctor to Mrs. White. Father went with her to visit him.

"Don't . . . feel bad for me, Virginia," said Ralph. He smiled weakly. "I . . . I'll be with our Lord soon!"

Virginia wiped a tear from her cheek and smiled back. "I love you, Ralph," she said, squeezing his hand.

"Steve," Ralph said to Father, "will they . . . let me see . . . your precious children?"

"I'll find out," promised Father.

With the doctor's permission, Father brought the children and Mother to the hospital a little later.

Ralph managed a smile as they entered the room. He lifted his hand from the bed and

motioned for the children to come closer.

"Please come . . . here . . . kids," he whispered.

Johnny, Joy, and Elaina walked to the edge of the bed. Ralph lifted his hand off the bed and Johnny took it in his own. Elaina and Joy moved in closer to Mr. White.

"You children have been . . . such cherished friends . . . to Virginia and me," said Ralph quietly. "Like . . . grandchildren . . . to us."

Ralph coughed and continued. "Do you . . . know what's happening to me?"

129

Johnny and Elaina sniffed and nodded their heads. But Joy didn't understand.

"Does your Mommy need to give you some medicine?" she asked.

Ralph smiled. "No, honey, medicine isn't . . . what I need anymore. I'm going to . . . to be with Jesus soon."

"When will you be back?" asked Joy.

Mr. White's eyes filled with tears.

"I . . . I won't be . . . coming back," he answered. "I'm going . . . to heaven . . . to live. The Bible says . . . I'll . . . be very happy there."

"We won't ever see you again!" said Elaina through her tears.

"No . . . that's not true," answered Ralph. "We . . . we'll all be together . . . with Jesus . . . someday." He closed his eyes, then reopened them and firmly grasped the children's hands in his own. He held up his hand and theirs in a victory salute.

"Praise you, Jesus," Ralph whispered. "Thank You . . . for taking me home!"

His hand dropped back to the bed. Ralph had gone to be with the Lord.

Check Your Head for What You've Read

1. Where did Ralph White say he was going to go to live after he died?

2. Did Ralph think he would be happy in heaven? What made him think so?

3. Who was Ralph going to be with in heaven? Who else will be there with him some day?

A Look Inside God's Special Book

After He had gone back to heaven to live with God the Father, Jesus sent a special message to His friend John. Jesus showed heaven to John and told him to write about what he saw. John was shown a wonderful new heaven and a new earth. He saw a new City of God, a city made of the purest gold and precious stones.

In this beautiful city there is no need for the sun and moon because it is lit by the goodness of God Himself! There is no hurting or death there, and no unhappiness at all—*ever*. God's people will live there with their Savior forever. It will be a much better, happier place than the earth could ever be!

Read more about heaven in Revelation 21–22.

When You Pray, Day by Day

Ask God:

• to help you see God's goodness always, even when someone you love dies
• to show you ways you can comfort people who have lost a loved one.

Thank God for the gift of life you enjoy and for the heavenly home that awaits all Christians someday.

Something Fun for Everyone

It is good to enjoy the life God has given you. What a wonderful gift! But it's also good to think about the wonders and beauty of heaven. It will be a terrific place!

Make a heavenly mobile.

Cut small pictures of things that remind you of heaven (for instance, gold, jewels, and maybe a beautiful building) out of magazines. Find a picture of Jesus in a Sunday school paper. Now draw a picture of your relatives who are already in heaven.

Take two sticks or dowels about eighteen inches long and connect them at their centers by wrapping a heavy string around them (make several wraps). Tie off the string. Attach another string, this one about two feet in length, where the sticks are joined. This string is for hanging the mobile.

Glue the pictures to construction paper. Cut them out and use a paper punch to make a hole in the top of each one. Attach threads of varying lengths to the pictures, and tie the other end of each thread to the crossed sticks. Now hang your mobile, and thank God for heaven and everyone who will be there!

God Will Take Care of Me
Trusting God in times of trouble

Johnny and Elaina took off their hats, coats, and mittens, and sat down on the couch in Mrs. White's living room.

"It's so nice of you to come today," she said with a smile. Mrs. White's eyes were puffy and red, and the children knew she had been crying. Her husband had died recently.

"We . . . we just wanted to see how you are doing, Mrs. White," said Johnny.

"Well, I miss Ralph very much, children," she answered, "but the Lord will take care of me."

"How do you know that?" asked Elaina.

"I've lived a long time," said Mrs. White. "God has done wonderful things in my life when times were difficult. I don't have any reason to doubt Him now."

"Mrs. White," said Johnny, "could you tell *us* about some of those things God has done for you?"

She smiled. "I'd be happy to," she answered. "You children may remember that my husband and I used to be missionaries. We lived for many years in a village in the mountains of Mexico.

"I remember one time when our food had run out and we had nothing to feed our four children," continued Mrs. White. "Life was hard in our little village at that time because there had been very little rain for several years.

"I was afraid our children might starve. But Ralph asked me to set the table as if we were going to have a feast. Then we sat down together, held each other's hands, and prayed."

"So what happened then?" asked Johnny.

"After the prayer," answered Mrs. White, "even before we had let go of each other's hands, someone knocked at the door. A man walking to our village had found a plump chicken wandering beside the road. He said he thought God had told him to give it to us!"

"Wow!" said Elaina. "God answered your prayer really fast!"

"Yes He did, Elaina," said Mrs. White. "But He wasn't finished yet. Not more than half an hour later, a wealthy landowner who lived nearby brought by a big sack of fruit

135

and vegetables, and enough corn meal to last a month! He had never been inside our mission, but said he'd suddenly had an urge to get to know his neighbors!"

"Will God listen to our prayers as hard as He listens to the prayers of missionaries, Mrs. White?" asked Johnny.

"Oh yes, children," she answered. "Trust Him to take care of your needs. Just *trust* Him. He hears every prayer—even if they're only whispered quietly in your heart.

"No one knows what is in store for us from one day to the next," Mrs. White continued. "But no matter how difficult things are, trust God to take care of you. I *know* He'll take care of me."

Check Your Head for What You've Read

1. Now that she is alone, is Mrs. White afraid of what might happen to her?
2. What happened when Mrs. White was a missionary that helps her trust God even now?
3. What did Mrs. White tell the children they should do when bad things happen to them?

A Look Inside God's Special Book

Job was a very wealthy man who honored God and hated evil. God allowed Satan to do many bad things to Job in order to test Job's faithfulness to God. Satan destroyed Job's many large flocks of animals, and most of his servants. And Satan made a house collapse with all of Job's children inside. They were killed.

Job felt horrible about the bad things that had happened. But did he turn from God? No! He said, "The Lord gave these things to me. And he has taken them away. Praise the name of the Lord."

Then Satan covered Job with painful sores. They were everywhere. But in spite of all his hardships, Job continued to love and trust God.

Find this story in Job 1–2.

When You Pray, Day by Day
Ask God:
- to help you trust Him even when your life is full of troubles
- to continue to provide for His missionaries, who trust God for everything they have every day.

Thank God for listening to your prayers, even the unspoken ones in your heart.

Something Fun for Everyone
Did you realize that the elderly people in your life are some of the wisest people you know? The longer we live, the more we learn about God and His goodness.

Do a "God Is Good" interview. Have you ever watched a newspaper or television news reporter conduct an interview? They may record a conversation with a tape recorder or a video recorder, but the person interviewing someone almost always has a notebook in hand. The interviewer writes on the notebook the most important things he or she learns in the interview.

Take a notebook and interview an older Christian–someone from your church, perhaps, or one of your grandparents. Ask that person to tell you about some difficult times in his or her life when God provided for the person's needs. Maybe the person was in need of food, money, or medical assistance. Ask if he or she prayed to God for help. How exactly *did* God help? Write down everything the person says about how God provided for his or her needs (you may need an adult's or older child's help with the writing). You may also want to record your interview on audio tape or videotape.

Thank the person you interview for giving you some real-life examples of how God loves us and provides for our needs. Then, afterward, share what you have learned with your family or Sunday school class! It may seem hard to trust God when there are troubles in your life, but remember: God *never* gives up on us, and we shouldn't give up on Him, either.

I Won't Give Her a Valentine
Being merciful

"This is fun, Mommy!" said Joy as she colored a heart she had drawn with a red marker.

It was late afternoon, and all the children Mother had watched during the day had already gone home with their parents. Joy was working at making Valentine's Day cards for her friends.

"Who is that one for?" asked Mother.

"This one is for Crystal," she answered. She made some swirls on the card with glue and sprinkled glitter on them.

139

"It's very pretty," said Mother with a smile. "And who is *that* one for–the one with the pretty flower on it?"

"It's for Rose," she answered. "That flower in the middle is a rose–and the girl hugging it is *me*."

"That will make Rose feel very special," said Mother.

"How about those two?" Mother asked, pointing to two look-alike valentines sitting side by side.

"They're for the Bradley twins," she answered.

"That's nice," said Mother. "I see you have one for each of the children I take care of during the day. No, that's not right– I don't see a valentine for Shira yet."

"Nope," Joy answered. "And I'm not *going* to make one for Shira."

"Well, it wouldn't be kind to give cards to all but *one* of your friends."

"She's not my friend," said Joy with a pout.

"Why do you say that?"

"She's mean to me," Joy answered. "She bosses me and always tries to take my toys away."

"Honey, we have to be especially nice to Shira right now," said Mother. "She's always been able to be home with her mommy before. But now her mommy has a job, and Shira is sad about that. Sometimes she shows her sadness by being naughty to other children."

"You mean I have to be nice to her even when she is *mean* to me?"

"Yes, Joy," said Mother as she slowly nodded her head. "Jesus taught that we should do good things to those who do bad things to us. And we need to pray for them."

"That sounds hard, Mommy," said Joy. "It's sure not what my *brain* says to do!"

Mother laughed. "Sometimes it's hard to do what Jesus wants us to do. But we obey Him anyway—out of love."

"So I need to make Shira a valentine?"

Mother nodded her head.

"Then I'll make a really pretty one," said Joy. "And I'll try to be extra nice to her, too."

Just then Elaina arrived home from school.

"Hi!" she said as she took off her hat and coat.

"Thursday is Valentine's Day, and I've got to get valentines done for all the kids in my class! All but Jeremy, that is. He's been really creepy, and I'm not going to give *him* a valentine."

"You and I need to have a talk," said Mother. She looked over at Joy and winked. Joy smiled at the little secret they shared.

Let's Rehearse a Bible Verse

Love your enemies. Do good to those who hate you.

Luke 6:27

141

Check Your Head for What You've Read

1. Why didn't Joy want to give Shira a valentine?
2. What reason did Mother give Joy for doing good to people who do bad things to us?
3. What was the secret Joy and Mother shared?
4. What do you think Mother told Elaina when they had *their* talk?

A Look Inside God's Special Book

Sometimes we don't know why we need to obey God. We just obey out of faith. Take Abraham, for example. God blessed Abraham and Sarah with a son. Abraham loved his son Isaac. So you can imagine how he felt when God told him to take Isaac to the mountains and kill him as a sacrifice!

It was the most difficult thing he'd ever had to do, but Abraham went to the mountains and built an altar there. He was about to take his son's life, when an angel stopped him. "Don't kill your son or hurt him in any way," said the angel. "Now I can see that you respect God." This had been a test of Abraham's faith, and Abraham passed the test. He had chosen to obey God—just because God *is* God.

Read this story in Genesis 22.

When You Pray, Day by Day
Ask God:

• to give you a desire to do good to people who are unkind to you, and to pray for them

• to show you how to be considerate of the feelings of others, and how to be aware of ways you can help someone who is unhappy.

Thank God for His gift of faith.

Something Fun for Everyone
Valentine's Day is a good time to remind people you care about them. But letting people know you love them is something you can do all year long.

Make a bunch of love stickers. First, buy a box of plain white stationery or note paper. On sheets of white paper, draw some hearts and other shapes with a thin-line black marker or pen. Using pastel watercolors (pink, yellow, green), color the shapes you have drawn.

When the sheets of stickers are dry, write some happy thoughts on some of them (*I love you; I care about you; I'm praying for you; Get well soon*). Now, using the recipe and instructions below, apply homemade glue to the back of the sheets.

Ingredients

8   tablespoons vinegar
4   packets of unflavored gelatin
1   tablespoon peppermint extract

Bring the vinegar to a boil and add the gelatin. Reduce heat to low, and stir until the gelatin is dissolved. Add the peppermint extract. Brush the glue on with a small paint brush. After the glue has dried, cut out your stickers. Whenever you find out someone is unhappy or sick, write that person an encouraging note, and decorate it with your stickers!

143

Father Has a Bad Morning

Confessing sin and asking for forgiveness

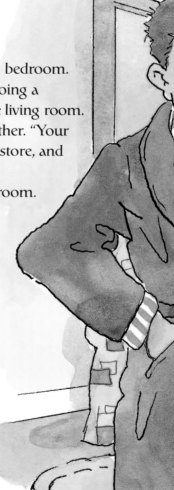

"Cut out all that noise!" yelled Father from his bedroom. It was Saturday morning, and the girls were doing a "fashion show" for Mother and Johnny in the living room.

"Let's be as quiet as possible, kids," said Mother. "Your father was up very late doing inventory at the store, and he needs more sleep."

A few minutes later, Father walked into the room.

"It's just about impossible to get any sleep around here," he grumbled.

"Good morning, Daddy!" said Elaina as she threw her arms around his waist. "Want to see our fashion show?"

"Not now, kids," said Father. "By the way, girls, I noticed a lot of clothes on the floor of your room when I walked down the hall. I'd like you to go put them away."

"But we're playing dress-up, Daddy," said Joy.

144

"I know what you're doing, but I don't think there's any reason for you to make such a mess of your bedroom," said Father. "So go clean it up."

The girls stared up at him with sad faces.

"Do it now!" Father said impatiently.

Then he went into the kitchen to get something to eat.

"Mom, have you seen my hat and mittens?" asked Johnny. "I'm ready to go to Champion's house, but can't find some of my things."

Before Mother could answer, Father came out of the kitchen and began talking to Johnny.

"You've lost your hat and mittens again?" he asked. "How many times have we told you to put them in the box by the door just as soon as you come in from outside?"

"I . . . I've been trying to remember to do that Dad, but–"

"Well, why don't you go to your room and think about it," said Father. Before Johnny walked away, Father thought he saw a tear in his son's eye.

"No, Johnny," said Father quietly. "Don't go to your room. I know you've been trying to keep track of your clothes. You've been doing much better. I'm sorry I snapped at you."

Father put his arms around Johnny and gave him a big hug. Then he called the girls back out into the room.

"I've been really crabby with you children this morning," began Father. "I've made all of *you* unhappy, and I've made *God* unhappy. Will you please forgive me?"

"I forgive you, Daddy," said Joy. Johnny and Elaina said they did also.

"Thanks, kids," said Father.

Turning to Mother, Father asked, "Will you forgive me too?"

"Of course I will," she said.

"I guess there's just one thing left to do," he said. Father asked everyone to hold hands while he prayed, asking God to forgive him.

After the prayer, the whole family searched until they found Johnny's missing hat and mittens. Then Father sat down on the couch beside Mother and watched a fashion show while he ate toast and drank coffee!

> ### Let's Rehearse a Bible Verse
>
> If we confess our sins, he will forgive our sins. . . .
> He will make us clean from all the wrongs we have done.
>
> 1 John 1:9

Check Your Head for What You've Read

1. What had Father done the night before that made him tired and crabby?

2. What did Father do that was wrong?

3. What happened when Father realized he had been wrong? Did his family forgive him? Do you think God forgave him too?

A Look Inside God's Special Book

Sometimes people are slow to confess the wrong things they do and to ask for forgiveness. Saul was like that. He hated Christians and went out of his way to harm them. One day, when Saul was on his way to Damascus to find and arrest Christians, he was blinded by a bright light from heaven. Then he heard the voice of Jesus say, "Saul, Saul! Why are you doing things against me?"

Jesus told Saul to go to Damascus, where someone would help him regain his sight. In Damascus, a man named Ananias laid his hands on Saul. Saul was filled with the Holy Spirit, he regained his sight, and he was baptized. He became a devoted servant of God!

Find this story in Acts 9.

When You Pray, Day by Day

Ask God:

• to help you forgive people who do wrong things to you

• to help you confess the bad things you have done, and to ask for forgiveness.

Thank God for taking away our sins and making us clean again when we ask Him to.

Something Fun for Everyone

Asking for forgiveness can be hard to do. But after you say you are sorry for what you have done and ask for forgiveness, you will know in your heart that God is pleased with you.

Build a Bible bookmark. A great way to remember the importance of asking for forgiveness is to make a bookmark for your Bible.

Take a colored, unlined 5- by 8-inch note card and fold it in half lengthwise. Cut along the crease, giving yourself two 8-inch-long card strips. (If you don't have any large note cards, use a smaller card or cut a strip out of a sheet of construction paper. If you use construction paper, you may want to cover your bookmark with clear contact paper after you finish it.)

Write these three things on your bookmark: (1) CONFESS SIN, (2) ASK FOR FORGIVENESS, and (3) THANK GOD. Remember each time you read those words to confess to God, and others, the wrong things you have done; then ask God and others to forgive you; and then thank God for His forgiveness.

Next, flip over the bookmark and write out the first part of the Bible verse for this week, 1 John 1:9: "If we confess our sins, he will forgive our sins." You can draw borders on your bookmark, flowers, or anything you like, if you have room. You may want to use a hole punch to make a small hole at the top of the bookmark. Thread a 10-inch-long piece of yarn through the hole and tie the ends of the yarn together.

When you cut a card in half to make your bookmark, you will have a strip of card left over. Why not make another bookmark and give it to a family member or friend?

TV Trouble
Keeping your heart pure

"Let's watch TV," suggested Brad to Johnny. They had been working on a homework project together since right after school.

"Sure," said Johnny. "I don't have to be home for a while yet. What should we watch?"

"I thought we could watch a video," Brad answered.

"What have you got?" asked Johnny.

"It's one my parents rented last night," he answered. "It's called *Nightmare in Hong Kong*."

"I need my parents' permission before I watch a video," Johnny said. "Let me look at the box."

Johnny read the label on the case and found out the film wasn't rated.

"I guess we can take a quick look and decide if it's OK or not," said Johnny.

Brad started the video. The opening scene was of a woman in a hotel room being killed by a man wearing a black mask.

"This looks *good*," said Brad. "Let's watch it."

"It looks scary to me," said Johnny. "I'll just watch a few minutes more to be sure it's one my parents would let me watch."

Johnny did watch for a few minutes. Then he watched a while longer. He often had to squeeze his eyes closed to shut out some horrible, bloody scenes. But there was no way he could close his ears to the outbursts of filthy language.

Before Johnny knew it, Brad's mother came to tell Johnny that Father was at the door. He had come to take Johnny home for dinner.

"How is your project coming?" Father asked as they drove home.

"Oh, fine," Johnny answered.

"Tell me about it," said Father.

"It's nothing special—just a history report." They drove the rest of the way home in silence.

Later that night, Father went to Johnny's room to tuck him into bed. "You've been very quiet tonight, son. Is something on your mind?"

Johnny just shook his head and looked away from his father's face.

"You must just be tired," Father said. "Let's pray so you can get right to sleep."

"I don't feel like praying tonight," said Johnny.

"Why not?" asked Father.

"Because . . . because I did something I shouldn't have today." A tear rolled down his cheek.

Father put his arm around Johnny. "Tell me about it, son. You'll feel better after you do."

Johnny told his father everything.

"Johnny, you already know what you did was wrong. That's why you don't want to pray tonight—because you're ashamed to face God." Johnny nodded his head.

"The Bible tells us we need to guard what goes into our mind," continued Father. "When we let bad things enter our mind, we become more and more like those bad things."

"I'm sorry, Dad," said Johnny. "I'd like to pray and ask God to forgive me."

Father gave Johnny's shoulder a squeeze. "I think that's a good idea," he said with a smile.

"And thanks for being honest with me tonight."

Let's Rehearse a Bible Verse

Create in me a pure heart, God. Make my spirit right again.

Psalm 51:10

Check Your Head for What You've Read

1. What should Johnny have done when Brad asked him if he wanted to watch a video?
2. Johnny broke a family rule when he watched a video without permission. But even without the rule, how could Johnny have been able to tell that the video was bad for him?
3. Why didn't Johnny want to pray at first?

A Look Inside God's Special Book

Jesus once talked about a farmer who went out to plant his field. Some seeds fell on the path and were eaten by birds. Some fell in rocky soil where they couldn't grow because of the rocks. Others fell among weeds. The weeds grew up and crowded the young plants out. But the seeds that fell into good soil, where there was no weeds or rocks, grew and produced a good crop.

Jesus explained the meaning of this story. He said the seed is the Good News about God. The birds, rocks, and weeds represent the things people allow into their hearts that keep them from God. But the good dirt is like the *pure hearts* of people who want to learn about God and love Him.

Read this story in Matthew 13.

When You Pray, Day by Day
Ask God:
• to help you resist the temptation to let bad things into your mind
• to give you the courage to confess your sins, so your heart can be made clean again.

Thank God for the seeds of Good News that are growing in your heart.

Something Fun for Everyone
All week long, think about ways you can keep your heart pure, so you will desire to seek and serve God.

Keep a "Pure Heart Journal." In a notebook or on a notepad, write down each day something you can do to guard your heart from bad things (foul language, bad lyrics in music on the radio, an inappropriate TV program, a DVD or video that shows things that don't honor God, and so on).

Entries in your journal might be similar to these:

• Wednesday—*Today I protected my heart against bad language when I refused to listen to a dirty joke.*

• Friday—*Some boys at school have been passing around a magazine that has pictures of naked people in it. I will guard my heart by leaving the room and not looking at the magazine if they ever offer it to me.*

At the end of the week, talk to your parents about what you have written in your journal. They may want to suggest other ways you can protect your heart and keep it pure for God.

Mystery in the Night
Learning to give happily

One night Johnny woke up with a start when he heard the squeal of tires and a loud *CRASH!* outside. He looked out his bedroom window and saw that a car had run into a huge tree across the street.

"Dad!" he yelled as he ran into his parents' bedroom. Father was already on his way outside to see if anyone had been hurt.

"That's the strangest thing!" said Father as he came back into the house. "The wrecked car is empty—there's no one inside. And it looks like Virginia White's car."

Father called the police. In a few minutes a police officer arrived.

"You say you think the car belongs to an elderly widow in the neighborhood?" said the policeman. "I'll check it out."

He went out to his car and made some calls on the radio.

"That car is a total loss," the policeman announced when he returned.

156

"And you were right, Mr. Kenton—it's registered to a Virginia White. I've sent an officer over to her house to talk with her."

"Please let us know if she needs any kind of help," said Father.

He called Mrs. White several minutes later, after allowing enough time for the police to talk with her.

"Some guy stole Virginia's car tonight," said Father after he hung up the phone. "Then he drove it into that tree and ran off."

"I feel so bad for her," said Mother.

"So do I. But there's more," Father said. "Her old car wasn't insured, and Virginia doesn't have enough money to buy another one."

Father made more phone calls the next morning, and then talked to Mother in the kitchen for a few minutes.

"Kids, we need to discuss something with you," said Mother when she and Father returned to the living room. "The church will help Mrs. White buy a car. But they can't get one for her for two weeks."

"Will she have to walk everywhere?" asked Joy.

"She's too old to do much walking," answered Father. "Your mother and I would like to rent her a car until she has one of her own. But now *we* have a problem."

"What is it?" asked Elaina.

"The only money we can use to rent a car right now is the money we've saved for the girls' new beds. If we help Mrs. White, Joy and Elaina will have to keep their bunk beds for a while."

"Oh, I don't *like* our bunk beds," wailed Elaina.

Let's Rehearse a Bible Verse

God loves the person who gives happily.

2 Corinthians 9:7

"Me either," added Joy.

"Girls, the money we have to spend was given to us by God," said Father. "God wants us to help others. And He wants us to do it happily."

No one spoke for a few moments.

"OK," said Joy finally, "let's help."

"Do you agree with that, Elaina?" asked Mother.

She had an undecided look on her face at first. Then she smiled. "Yes," she said. "Let's help Mrs. White today!"

Check Your Head
for What You've Read

1. What caused the loud noise that woke Johnny and his parents?
2. What problem did Mrs. White have after the accident? Was she able to solve it alone?
3. What did Mother and Father suggest that the Kentons do to help Mrs. White? Did the girls agree? Did they do it happily?

A Look Inside God's Special Book

What we *think* about our giving–our attitude–is very important. One day Jesus was in God's temple where He was watching people give money for God's work. Many rich people put large amounts of money into the collection box. Then a poor widow came along and put two small coins into the box. These coins were worth very little.

Jesus called His followers over and told them that the widow had really given much *more* than the rich people gave. "The rich have plenty; they gave only what they did not need," said Jesus. "This woman is very poor. But she gave all that she had. . . ." The woman's gift was a true sacrifice made out of love for God.

Find this story in Mark 12 and Luke 21.

When You Pray, Day by Day
Ask God:
• to help you be willing to give to people who are in need of your help
• to give you a happy heart when you give to others.
Thank God that His people want to help meet the needs of others–even *your* needs.

Something Fun for Everyone
There are many ways we can give to others. The following activity will help you think of some.

• **Read a book about giving.** *Charlotte's Web,* by E. B. White, will show you a new way to look at what giving and friendship are all about. You can find this book in your public library.

• **Make a giving tree.** On a piece of green construction paper, trace around your hand several different times. Cut these shapes out. (They will be the branches and leaves of your tree.) Now cut a tree trunk out of brown construction paper.

Next, think of ways you can give to others, and write these down on your "branches." For example, you can give your belongings, money, and time (cutting the grass, raking leaves, reading to someone). Write the word GIVING on the trunk. Glue your tree together on a sheet of white construction paper.

SPRING

March
April
May

Easter (Weeks 3 and 4)

Unexpected Ski Vacation
Learning to cooperate

"Kids, your mother and I would like to talk to you," said Father. "Uncle Richard called today. He reserved a cabin for some late-season skiing this weekend, but he needs to take a business trip instead. The reservation is already paid, so he asked if we would like to go."

"Yip-pee!" said Johnny. "But . . . it's spring now. There hasn't been any snow for *weeks*."

"Not around here there hasn't," agreed Mother. "But there still is plenty in the mountains."

"The mountains are hundreds of miles away," he said. "Wouldn't we be driving all weekend?"

"It's a long drive, all right," said Father. "That's why we hope to leave Wednesday morning— the day after tomorrow. But we can do that *only* if we get a lot done between now and then."

"Will we get out of school to go on the trip?" asked Elaina hopefully.

"Yes, you will," said Mother. "But you'll have to get all of your assignments from your teachers and take your homework with you. Besides taking care of homework assignments, we'll also need other kinds of cooperation from each of you to make this work."

"What's cop . . . copper-*ra*-tion," asked Joy, having a hard time with the big word.

"Cooperation is working together as a team to get a job done," answered Father. "You'll all need to help us get ready to go."

That evening and the next day were a blur of activity at the Kenton house. Everyone packed and made arrangements to have friends take care of things while they were gone.

165

The family got up early on Wednesday morning. They still had lots to do before they could start their trip.

"I want you children to make your beds and straighten your rooms now," said Mother.

"Do we have to?" complained Johnny.

"It will only take a few minutes if you work quickly," she answered. "Then I'd like you to vacuum the living room, Johnny, while Elaina makes sandwiches and snacks for the trip. Joy needs to find her blanket and teddy bear and give them to Daddy so he can load them in the car."

"You mean all Johnny has to do is vacuum, and I have to make all those sandwiches and stuff?" asked Elaina. "I have more work to do than he does!"

"When Johnny is done with the vacuuming, he needs to help Father load the car," said Mother.

"Then *I'll* be doing more than Elaina!" said Johnny.

"Let's stop this right now," said Mother sternly. "Do you think Jesus is happy with all this complaining? We *all* have jobs to do. If anyone doesn't do his or her job, it hurts all of us. Do you think we can all agree again to cooperate?"

Johnny and Elaina looked sorry for making a fuss over such little things.

"I'm sorry, Mom," said Johnny.

"Me too, Mommy," agreed Elaina.

With no more complaints, everyone went to work.

167

Check Your Head for What You've Read

1. Why did the Kentons suddenly get to go skiing?
2. What did they all need to do in order to get ready for the trip?
3. What were Johnny and Elaina complaining about? How does Jesus feel when we complain?

A Look Inside God's Special Book

Moses led the Israelites to the land God had promised them, then he sent twelve spies out to explore the land. Two of the spies, Caleb and Joshua, reported that the land was very good and ready for them to take for their own. But the other spies gave a bad report about the land, saying they would all die if they tried to take it.

That night the Israelite people began complaining. "Why is the Lord bringing us to this land?" they asked. God was angry about the complaints of His people and their lack of faith. As punishment, the Israelites were not allowed to enter the promised land for another forty years—until after all the adults had died. Only Caleb and Joshua lived to enter the land!

Find this story in Numbers 13–14.

When You Pray, Day by Day

Ask God:

• to help you develop an attitude of cooperation

• to help you do your jobs around the house without complaining or arguing.

Thank God for being good to us even when we blow it and aren't thoughtful of Him.

Something Fun for Everyone

Getting ready for trips can be a king-size hassle, or it can be a nearly hassle-free experience—if you prepare ahead of time. The following project can make trip preparation easy and fun!

Make a Suitcase Travel List.

First, you will need a sturdy piece of white poster board that measures about eleven by seventeen inches. Neatly fold it in half. Now cut out a pair of poster board suitcase handles and attach them with glue or staples. Write "Travel List" on both handles.

From old catalogs and magazines, cut pictures of things you will need to pack when you go on a trip (for example: clothes, homework, Bible, diary, toothbrush and personal items, travel games). Glue these pictures onto the inside of your suitcase. (You may simply want to write out your list inside the suitcase.) Color the outside of the suitcase. Keep your list and use it every time you travel!

Note: You may want your mother or father to keep your list for you. (Tell them it will fit inside a file cabinet just like a file folder—and the handle will help them find it easily!)

A Friendship Blooms
Learning not to covet

The Kenton family was on a spring skiing vacation.
Elaina and Johnny were taking ski lessons together.
Joy was with Father on the "Bunny Hill" for beginners,
and Mother was at the lodge, where she planned
to read and relax while the others skied.

"I sure wish I had a fancy outfit like *she* has," Elaina
said to Johnny. She pointed to a girl nearby who
was wearing bright, colorful clothes. She also had
new-looking skis. Elaina was wearing her warm
winter clothes, but she didn't own any stylish
clothing for the slopes.

"And I just hate these beat-up old skis,"
she added. "I wish we didn't always have
to rent skis. I'd like to have my own."

"We don't ski often enough to
need all that fancy stuff," said Johnny.

Later, Father and the children sat
outside in the warm spring
sunshine. They were eating the

lunches Mother had packed for them that morning.

Elaina whispered to Johnny, "Why can't we eat in that restaurant over there, where everyone else is having lunch? Why do we always take our lunches with us when we go places?"

Just then Elaina noticed a little girl with long brown braids sitting a couple of tables over from them. She appeared to be about Elaina's age and was eating a sandwich, just like Elaina was.

"Hi," said Elaina. "Are you here to ski?"

"No," said the girl. "My mother is a cook in the restaurant. I'm on my lunch break from school. Mom is going to meet me here."

"Wow!" said Elaina. "You really *live* here? You must get to ski all the time!"

"No," she said, "I've never skied before. We don't have enough money for that. But I'm very lucky that God gave my parents jobs here. I love the snow and mountains. And it's fun to watch the skiers come down the hill. From here they look like ants on an ice cream cone!"

Elaina went back to eating her lunch. She suddenly felt bad for wanting the things other people had. She turned to Father.

"Daddy? Would you mind if I asked that girl if she would like to use my equipment and have my lift ticket and ski lesson tomorrow?"

"No, sweetie," he answered. "That's very kind. But tomorrow is Saturday–our last day for skiing. Are you sure you want to give it up?"

"I've already had lots of fun skiing, Daddy. I'd like to share with her. I think Jesus would like me to do it too. I can spend the day with Mommy."

"I'm proud of you, honey," said Father.

The brown-haired girl's mother came out and sat with her daughter. Father and Elaina went over to talk with them. Soon they were all smiling and laughing together. Elaina had made a new friend very happy.

Let's Rehearse a Bible Verse

Keep your lives free from the love of money.
And be satisfied with what you have.

Hebrews 13:5

173

Check Your Head for What You've Read

1. What was Elaina unhappy about?

2. What helped Elaina to realize that she should be happy with what she had?

3. Why did the little girl Elaina met outside the restaurant feel that she was lucky?

4. What did Elaina do for this little girl? Why was that a good thing to do?

A Look Inside God's Special Book

After Moses led the Israelites out of slavery in Egypt, they camped at the foot of Mount Sinai. God had come to the mountain to give Moses a list of rules that He wanted the Israelites to obey. One of the things God said the Israelites shouldn't do was *covet*—which means to want what belongs to someone else.

"You must not covet your neighbor's wife," God told Moses to tell the Israelite people. "You must not covet his wife or his men or women slaves. You must not want to take anything that belongs to your neighbor."

It makes God happy when we are satisfied with what He has given us.

Read more about this story in Exodus 19–20.

When You Pray, Day by Day
Ask God:
• to help you be satisfied with what you have
• to give you opportunities to help people who have less than you do.
Thank God for all the good things He has given you to use and to share.

Something Fun for Everyone
Did you ever wish you could share with others on a regular basis? A way to do that is to start a personal or family ministry. Talk over with your parents the following ministry ideas.

• **Write letters to servicemen.** Men and women in our country's armed forces would welcome a letter of encouragement from you. Let these people know God loves them.

• **Do yard work and odd jobs for the elderly and shut-ins.** If you and your family know of some elderly people who live in their own homes, offer to help them with jobs they can't easily do themselves.

• **Help people who are handicapped.** Do you know people at school or somewhere else who are in a wheelchair, or blind, or who can't hear? Find out how you can help them. (You can do errands for them, read to them, write letters for them, or just be their friend!)

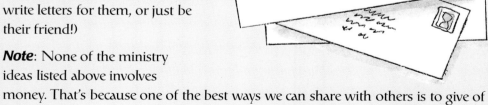

Note: None of the ministry ideas listed above involves money. That's because one of the best ways we can share with others is to give of our time.

An Easter Opportunity

Serving others with love

"I have some news, kids!" said Father as he arrived home from work. "Our church will be serving Easter dinner to the people who live at Crestview nursing home. I've signed up our family to help."

"What would there be for kids to do?" asked Johnny. "We'd probably just be in the way."

"Not at all," said Mother. "You can help set tables, get things for people that we've forgotten to put out . . . and just *talk* to people. Most nursing home residents love children."

"But I *hate* nursing homes," announced Elaina. "We don't know anyone, and those old people are always patting us on the head and trying to hug us. *Ugh!*"

"Those places smell bad, too," added Joy.

"Look, kids," said Father. "Let's not forget about the good we can do there . . . the things we can do for *Jesus.*

"Many nursing home residents are very lonely and don't get a lot of visitors," he continued. "But even more important, some of them don't know Jesus yet. Don't you think it would be a good idea to show those people some of Jesus' love?"

"I . . . I guess we should," said Elaina. She didn't look very happy.

176

On Easter morning the Kenton family got up early and went to a special sunrise Easter service. It was held outdoors on a hilltop outside of town. Next came a big breakfast at the church, followed by the regular Easter service. There was so much to do on Easter!

"Come on, kids, we have to hurry to get to the nursing home," said Mother after church.

"Remember, children," said Father, "we want people to see Jesus in us today."

In the nursing home dining room, the Kentons and the other helpers worked hard. Johnny and Elaina put silverware and napkins on tables. Father and some of the other men and women set out the food.

Mother and Joy worked at filling little Easter baskets with treats for the nursing home residents. Mother smiled as Joy every once in a while popped a chocolate Easter egg into her mouth!

Soon the Crestview residents began to enter the room. A nursing home worker pushed a very old lady in a wheelchair up to a table where Elaina was just putting out a basket full of dinner rolls.

"Well, aren't you a little cutie?" said the lady. Elaina tried to smile when the old woman gave her a pat on the head.

"My name is Elvie Wilson," said the woman. "What's your name, sweetheart?"

Elaina looked a little embarrassed.

"Uh . . . it's Elaina. Elaina Kenton."

"You remind me *so* much of my great-granddaughter," said Elvie. "I thank God that you folks came to be with us today."

Elaina saw tears of happiness forming in Elvie Wilson's eyes. Suddenly Elaina leaned forward and gave Elvie a big hug.

"I'm glad we came too," she said with a smile.

Let's Rehearse a Bible Verse

The Son of Man did not come for other people to serve him. He came to serve others. The Son of Man came to give his life to save many people.

Matthew 20:28

Check Your Head for What You've Read

1. Why didn't the Kenton children want to help serve Easter dinner at the nursing home?

2. Why did Father think it was important for the family to help serve dinner to the nursing home residents?

3. What changed Elaina's mind about receiving pats on the head and hugs from the people at the nursing home?

A Look Inside God's Special Book

A short time before Jesus was put to death on the cross, He had dinner with some special friends, His disciples. During the meal, Jesus got up, wrapped a towel around His waist, and began washing His friends' feet. He dried their feet with the towel He wore around His waist. But Peter said he couldn't allow Jesus to wash *his* feet.

So Jesus explained to Peter and His other friends why it was important for Him to do this. He said, "I, your Lord and Teacher, have washed your feet. So you also should wash each other's feet. I did this as an example for you. So you should do as I have done." Jesus was saying that one mark of a Christian is that he or she will be willing to *serve others*.

Find this story in John 13.

When You Pray, Day by Day

Ask God:

• to help you see the possible good things in a situation, rather than the bad

• to give you a desire to serve others, just as Jesus would.

Thank God for becoming a man and showing us how to live good lives.

Something Fun for Everyone

Wouldn't it be great to find a way to serve others, spread the Good News of salvation, and have fun—all at the same time? You can!

Have a Good News Easter Egg Hunt. Buy a bag or two of large plastic eggs—the kind that come apart (they're available in many stores). Cut sheets of paper into strips about an inch wide.

On the paper strips, write Easter messages about Jesus. Some examples: "Jesus loves you." "Jesus died that we can have eternal life." "Serve the Lord with gladness in your heart." "On the third day He arose." Also include Scripture verse references on some of these slips of paper *(don't write out the verses)*. Some examples are: John 3:16, John 11:25, Job 19:25, John 8:12, John 10:11, and Ephesians 6:1.

Put a slip of paper in each egg, hide the eggs, and invite neighborhood friends over for a Good News egg hunt! After the eggs have been collected, have everyone read their messages aloud. Look up all the Scripture references in the Bible and read them, too.

Note: You can have a Good News egg hunt any time of year!

The Miracle of Easter
Remembering the sacrifice of Jesus

The meal that the Kenton family and others had served to the nursing home residents had been a big success.

As the adults cleared dishes off the tables, the children passed out Easter baskets. Mother and Joy had filled the baskets with plastic grass, candy Easter eggs, chocolate bunnies, and yellow marshmallow chicks.

After the children passed out all the baskets, Elaina took Johnny and Joy over to meet a new friend of hers.

"This is Elvie Wilson," began Elaina. "She said she wants to meet both of you." Elaina introduced Johnny and Joy to Mrs. Wilson.

"It's so nice of all of you to come today," said Elvie. "Easter is such a special time. . . ."

"Yes!" agreed four-year-old Joy. "We get chocolate eggs and Easter bunnies, and hunt eggs!"

"Those are a fun part of our celebration of Easter," said Mrs. Wilson, "but what does Easter really *mean* to us?"

"It means Jesus came alive again," said Elaina.

"That's right," said Elvie. "When Jesus came back to life it proved to the world that He was who He said He was—the *Son of God*. But why did He have to die in the first place?"

182

"Because of sin," said Johnny.

"Whose sin?" she asked.

"*Everybody's* sin, I guess," answered Johnny. "Jesus died for the sins of the people who lived when *He* did, and He died for our sins, too."

"That's right," said Elvie. "As I've grown older, I find myself thinking more and more about how much I love Jesus. I've done lots of wrong things in my long life. But I'm clean inside and forgiven because Jesus was punished and died *in my place.*

183

"That's the miracle of Easter to me, children—that I am forgiven of my sins because Jesus took my punishment for me. He loved me enough to die for me. And He loves each of *you* that much too.

"He's so precious to me, children," Elvie continued. "I hope Jesus will always be precious to each of you, too. Don't forget what the cross really means. Please don't ever forget. . . ."

The children talked with Elvie for another hour. She told them about her family and her favorite Easter memories. When she was a little girl, Elvie rode to Easter services in a big wagon pulled by a horse. Few people had cars where she lived at that time.

Elaina, Joy, and Johnny told Elvie about school, their friends, the sports they liked, and many other things. Elvie seemed interested in everything they said. Finally, Mother and Father came over and told the children it was time to go.

"I just love your children," Elvie told their parents. "I've enjoyed our visit today so *very* much!"

Let's Rehearse a Bible Verse

This is how God showed his love to us: He sent his only Son into the world to give us life through him.

1 John 4:9

"Kids, would you like to come back and visit Mrs. Wilson again soon?" asked Father.

All three said they would.

Check Your Head for What You've Read

1. What did Mrs. Wilson and the children decide is the real meaning of Easter?
2. What did Mrs. Wilson mean when she talked about the "miracle of Easter"?
3. Do you think the children enjoyed their visit to the nursing home? Why do you think so?

A Look Inside God's Special Book

Jesus doesn't want us to forget why He died on the cross. One evening Jesus was having a special dinner with His twelve disciples. While they were eating, He took some bread, thanked God for it, and broke it. Then He gave it to His disciples and said, "Take this bread and eat it. This bread is my body."

Next, Jesus took a cup and thanked God for it, then gave it to His disciples. "Every one of you drink this," He said. "This is my blood which begins the new agreement that God makes with his people. This blood is poured out for many to forgive their sins." Jesus died so that our sins could be forgiven.

Read more about this in Matthew 26.

When You Pray, Day by Day
Ask God:
• to help you never forget why Jesus died on the cross
• to give you a love for Jesus that grows bigger every day.

Thank God for loving us so much that He sent Jesus to earth, so that we can have life forever.

Something Fun for Everyone
Sometimes when people get old, they go to nursing homes where people can give them the special care they need. These people need to be loved as much as ever, but some of them become very lonely in these homes.

Adopt a nursing-home resident. Like the Kenton children in this week's story, you can make a new friend in a nursing home. (If you have a relative in a nursing home, you can become a better friend to that relative.) In fact, you can "adopt" a shut-in, an old person in your neighborhood, a person with a handicap—anyone who needs love.

Do you like art? Share your paintings and drawings with your new friend. Do you like to read? Read for your friend. If you're a good talker, just spend time visiting with your friend. It's not important how you share with another person—your willingness to share shows your love.

Note: If personal visits aren't possible, you can share with a friend by mail—such things as letters, photos, and artwork. You can also make audio recordings on cassette tapes or make fun videos with a video camera!

187

She Makes Me So Mad!
Dealing with anger

Joy and the children Mother cared for during the day were seated around a big table, drawing pictures.

The Bradley twins were making pictures of scary animals. Crystal was drawing pretty spring flowers. And Rose was making a picture of her brother playing baseball on a bright sunny day.

Joy found a picture in a magazine of a long-haired orange and white kitten. She began to draw the cat. Because Shira hadn't yet decided what she would draw, she peeked over Joy's shoulder.

"You're not doing that right," she told Joy. "I'll show you how to draw that kitten."

Joy didn't like being told she wasn't doing a good job—especially by Shira—so she went right ahead with her picture.

"I can't see that magazine picture good enough," said Shira. "Give it here." Shira grabbed the magazine and put it right next to her paper.

"No!" shouted Joy. "I'm using it now!" Joy yanked the magazine back.

"I think you both can see the magazine if you put it in the middle," said Mother. She moved it so that both girls could see.

Joy had just finished coloring her kitten's fluffy orange tail when Shira leaned over to check Joy's progress.

"Oh, that's ugly!" said Shira. "You're still doing it wrong. Here, look . . . I did it the *right* way."

Shira held her drawing up under Joy's nose, and before Mother could stop her, Joy grabbed Shira's picture and ripped it in half!

"I don't care about your dumb cat!" said Joy. She ran out of the room to her bedroom.

Mother got Shira another sheet of paper, then went to the bedroom to talk with Joy.

"Joy, there's no reason to let your anger get the best of you that way," began Mother. "You shouldn't have torn Shira's picture."

"But she makes me so mad!" said Joy.

"I know she does, honey," answered Mother. "But you need to look beyond the bad things she does and try to love her. Let me read something from the Bible.

"This is found in Colossians 3: 'Do not be angry with each other, but forgive each other. If someone does wrong to you, then forgive him. Forgive each other because the Lord forgave you.' Paul goes on to say that the most important thing we can do is love each other."

"But how can I forgive and love someone who isn't nice to me?" Joy asked.

Let's Rehearse a Bible Verse

Do not be bitter or angry or mad. Never shout angrily or say things to hurt others. Never do anything evil.

Ephesians 4:31

"You need to pray and ask for Jesus' help," Mother answered.

"Can you teach me how to pray like that?" asked Joy.

"Sure I can, sweetie," her mother answered. "And when we're done, you need to go ask Shira to forgive *you* for tearing up her picture."

Joy slowly nodded her head in agreement.

Check Your Head for What You've Read

1. Why was Joy angry with Shira?

2. Did Mother think it was OK for Joy to tear up Shira's drawing? What reason did Mother give?

3. What did Mother say to help Joy learn to forgive and love Shira?

A Look Inside God's Special Book

Do you remember how Jacob tricked his brother Esau and stole their father Isaac's blessing? Esau was so angry that he wanted to kill Jacob. So Jacob ran away to a distant land. His uncle lived there, and Jacob hoped to find a wife there among his own people.

The Lord richly blessed Jacob in the land of his uncle. Jacob had wives, many children, and flocks of animals. He became very rich. One day Jacob decided to return to his homeland, but he was afraid. Would Esau still want to kill him, and maybe his family too? Jacob prayed to God for protection. When Esau saw Jacob, he threw his arms around him and hugged him. God had helped Esau forgive Jacob for what he had done!

Find this story in Genesis 27–28 and 32.

When You Pray, Day by Day
Ask God:
• to help you keep your anger under control
• to enable you to forgive people who are unkind to you.
Thank God for the power of prayer and forgiveness.

Something Fun for Everyone
Often it's hard to know how to respond to others when they do wrong things to us. But the Bible can guide our responses in these situations.

Take a "How Do I Respond When . . ." quiz. Don't worry, this isn't really a quiz—it's an activity that can help you respond like God wants when someone has done something wrong to you. Look up the Scripture references listed, then think about (or discuss) what God would want you to do in each situation below.

• Leviticus 19:17–18 • Matthew 5:7 • Matthew 5:39–47 • Matthew 5:44
• Matthew 18:21–22 • Luke 6:35–36 • Romans 12:19
• Romans 12:17–21 • 1 Corinthians 4:12

How should I respond:
• when someone hurts me
• when someone makes fun of me
• when someone steals from me
• when someone hates me
• when someone lies about me
• when someone swears at me
• when someone has done something bad to me over and over again

Did you say God wants us to forgive the other person in each situation above? *You're right!*

Trouble with the Big Boys
Dealing with peer pressure

"Hey, Caleb, wait for me!" said Johnny as he hurried to catch up with his neighbor, Caleb Smith, on their way home from school.

"Hi, Johnny. What's up?" asked Caleb.

195

"Nothing special," Johnny answered. "I thought I might see you at Little League tryouts last night. Aren't you going to play ball this year?"

"Naw," answered Caleb. "My friends aren't interested in stuff like that, so I guess I'm not either."

"Caleb . . ." began Johnny carefully, "I've noticed you're spending a lot of time with Donny Jacobs lately. He and his friends have been in lots of trouble, and they're all a year or two older than us. . . . Maybe you shouldn't hang out with them so much."

"I can take care of myself . . ." said Caleb.

The boys said good-bye when they got to Johnny's house. Caleb walked on home alone.

When Caleb reached his house, he found Donny Jacobs and one of Donny's friends, Max Thompson, waiting for him in the yard. Caleb didn't know his real name, but he knew "Max" had gotten his nickname by being big for his age. He also was known as a bully.

"Grab your bike and come to town with us," said Donny.

"Sure," Caleb answered. "Mom and my brother won't be home for a while, so I've got time to kill."

Once up town, the boys parked their bikes and began wandering through stores.

"Hey, check *these* out," said Max as

he examined a fancy pair of sunglasses he'd picked up off a rack in a store. "I'd look great in these, guys," he said, giving Caleb a playful jab in the ribs with his elbow. Caleb smiled, and Donny nodded his head in approval.

To Caleb's surprise, Max turned his head to the left and to the right, then dropped the glasses into his coat pocket. Donny smiled.

"I think I'd look good in *this* pair," said Donny as he picked up a pair of glasses. "Yeah, these are all right." He left the glasses on. "I think that pair would look good on Caleb," Donny said, pointing.

Max reached over, took the glasses off the rack, and roughly

197

pushed them on Caleb's nose.

"N-no, thanks. I don't need sunglasses right now, Max," Caleb said.

"Donny, I think Caleb is a *scaredy-cat!*" Max hissed in a loud whisper.

"I am not!" said Caleb. "I'll keep the dumb glasses."

The boys headed for the door. When they were outside, a man from the store stopped them.

"That's far enough, boys," he said. "Come back inside so we can talk."

"Let's get out of here!" said Donny.

The boys took off, running down the street. But Caleb couldn't keep up with the older boys. Suddenly he felt a hand on his shoulder.

Two hours later, Johnny saw a police car cruise slowly up his street. It stopped at Caleb's house.

I wonder what <u>that's</u> all about, thought Johnny.

Check Your Head for What You've Read

1. Why was Johnny worried about the friendship Caleb had with Donny and his friends?

2. Why did Caleb decide to steal the glasses?

3. What do you think happened to Caleb after he was caught? Did his friends stay to help him?

A Look Inside God's Special Book

Sometimes we do things we shouldn't do because a friend or someone else talks us into doing them. This first happened at the beginning of the world when Satan talked Eve into eating fruit from the tree of the knowledge of good and evil. God had told Adam and Eve that they must never do that.

Once Eve had eaten this fruit, she talked Adam into eating some. God said to Adam, "You listened to what your wife said. And you ate fruit from the tree that I commanded you not to eat from." So God punished Adam and Eve. He made them leave the beautiful garden. And He said that from that time on, men would have to work very hard for their food, and there would be pain and death in the world. Adam and Eve (and all the people who came after them, including us) paid a big price for their sin.

Find out more about this in Genesis 3.

199

When You Pray, Day by Day
Ask God:
• to help you know how to deal with the pressure of people who want you to do wrong things
• to give you the wisdom to choose good friends.
Thank God for being a true friend—one who will always help you when you are in need.

Something Fun for Everyone
When someone tries to get you to do something wrong, your first defense should be to *pray*. Ask God to give you the strength to say no.

Role-play ways to say no. It may help to practice ahead of time what to say in different situations. Look at the situations and responses on the next page. Pretend you are being pressured to do something wrong, and practice saying the responses provided.

If you don't let me copy your homework, you're no friend of mine. . . .
It's wrong to be dishonest. If I did this, I would dishonor myself *and* God.

It's OK for you to take a few puffs of this cigarette. . . .
I don't want to hurt my body. God says my body is the temple of God.

Your mother will never miss that money. Go ahead and take it. . . .
It's wrong to steal and to lie. The Bible says so, my parents say so, and I know it's true!

Ask your parents to help you think of other role-playing situations and responses. Talk together about why it is a good idea to know how to respond when someone tries to get you to do something you shouldn't do.

A Real Friend
Forming godly friendships

"Hello?" said Johnny as he answered the phone. "Oh, hi, Caleb . . . Yes, I'll be home—come on over."

A few minutes later, Johnny heard a knock at the front door. As he let Caleb in, he noticed that he looked troubled.

Johnny got two big glasses of lemonade from the kitchen, and the boys went outside to sit on the back steps in the warm afternoon sunshine.

"I owe you an apology," began Caleb.

"Apology? Apology for what?"

"Yesterday you warned me that Donny Jacobs and his friends were bad news, but I didn't listen. It made me feel good to hang around with them. But now I know you were only trying to keep me from the kind of trouble that I got into yesterday afternoon."

"What happened?"

Caleb looked away from Johnny and didn't answer at first. "I'm afraid you won't like me anymore if I tell you," he said finally.

"That's not true. You'll still be my friend, no matter what you've done."

"OK, I'll tell you," said Caleb. "I went to town with Donny and Max Thompson. They talked me into stealing a pair of sunglasses. They both stole a pair too. I guess I wouldn't be apologizing now except that I got caught—and they ran away!"

"What happened after you were caught?" asked Johnny.

"First the store manager said a lot of things to me about being a thief," answered Caleb. "He didn't believe me when I told him I'd never done it before. He said he recognized the guys I was with, and that if I was *their* friend, I had probably been stealing all over town. Then he called the police."

Let's Rehearse a Bible Verse

A friend loves you all the time.

Proverbs 17:17

"I'm sorry all this happened, Caleb," said Johnny.

"So am I," Caleb sighed. "The policeman questioned me and said I probably would wind up in jail someday! Then he took me home and talked to Mom. She cried for a long time.

"Johnny, this has all been so horrible!" Caleb continued. "I'm sorry I hurt my mom, and I know I hurt God too. What do you think I should do?"

Johnny thought for a minute and said a silent prayer, asking God for help. Then he put his arm on Caleb's shoulder.

"First of all," said Johnny, "I think you need to know that your mom still loves you. God does too. The Bible says we will be forgiven of the wrong things we do when we pray and confess them and try to do what's right.

"I also think it might be good for you to learn more about the Bible," said Johnny.

"Yeah, I know I need to," answered Caleb. "I've been going to Sunday school for a while, but there still is so much I need to learn."

"I belong to an after-school Bible club," said Johnny. "We get together once a week to read and memorize Scripture. Would you like to go with me next week?"

"You bet I would!" said Caleb. "And Johnny—thanks for being a *real* friend to me."

Check Your Head for What You've Read

1. Why did Caleb apologize to Johnny?

2. Why do you think neither the store manager nor the policeman believed that Caleb hadn't ever stolen anything before?

3. What did Johnny suggest that Caleb do to start making things right?

A Look Inside God's Special Book

True friendship runs deep. After David had killed Goliath, King Saul made David an important man in the kingdom. David became a very good friend of Saul's son, Jonathan. David was made a leader of the armies of Israel, and he became famous.

Saul grew jealous of David. He was afraid people would want David to be king. So Saul decided to kill him. Jonathan couldn't believe his father wanted to kill David, but he told David, "If I learn that my father plans to harm you, I will warn you!" When he found out David *was* in great danger, Jonathan warned David and sent him away. But first they promised to remain friends forever.

Read more about this story in 1 Samuel 18–20.

When You Pray, Day by Day
Ask God:
• to show you how to be a good friend to others
• to bring friends into your life who will be there for you when you are in need.
Thank God for all the wisdom in the Bible, and for how the Bible can help you live a good life.

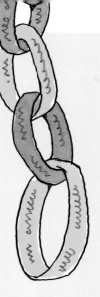

Something Fun for Everyone
True friendship with someone is like being bound to that person with a chain, a chain of goodness.

Make a friendship chain. It's good to remind ourselves of what being a real friend is all about. Cut a couple of sheets of colored construction paper into strips at least eight inches long by one inch wide. Write the following features of true friendship on the strips, leaving a margin of at least an inch at both ends of the strip.
• A friend is kind.
• A friend is willing to sacrifice for another.
• A friend always tries to believe the best about the other person.
• A friend is faithful.
• A friend is trusting *and* trustworthy.
• A friend will correct another only in love.
• A friend will offer good advice.
• A friend loves unconditionally–without strings attached.
• A friend will pray for another often.

Can you think of other characteristics of a good friend? Write them down too. Using glue or staples, make a chain with the strips of paper. Hang it from a bulletin board or a wall, and pull off one link a day as a reminder.
Note: You can keep the chain links in a long envelope after you remove them from the chain.

A King-size Misunderstanding

Avoiding hasty conclusions

Elaina stood back and admired the fort she and Johnny had built out of a big blue tarp. Just then Father arrived home from work.

"Dad!" she called out. "Come look at our fort!"

"I can't right now, sweetie," he answered. "Ron Davis is picking me up in five minutes so we can get in a quick game of tennis before dinner."

"Sometimes Dad doesn't seem to care much about us kids," said Johnny as Elaina climbed underneath the tarp to join him. "I'll bet he's forgotten he promised to spend the day with us tomorrow."

That evening after dinner, Johnny overheard the last few words of a telephone conversation.

"Thanks," Father said to someone. "I know we'll have a fun day. I'll meet you at 7:30 tomorrow morning at the clubhouse."

Later, after the children had been tucked in bed, Johnny sneaked into the girls' room.

"Guess what Dad is doing tomorrow," he said. "He's going to play golf!"

"Are you sure?" asked Elaina.

"I heard him set it up!" said Johnny.

The children were up early the next morning. They looked out the bedroom window and saw Father climb into the car and leave.

"There!" said Johnny. "Do you believe me now?"

Both girls slowly nodded their heads.

"If Daddy doesn't like us anymore," began Joy, "I guess we'll have to get a *new* daddy."

Johnny thought for a moment.

"No," he said, "we can't do that. But we don't have to stay here, either. Let's go visit Uncle Mark! He always has time to spend with us."

"How will we get there?" asked Elaina.

"We'll hitchhike," he answered. "I've seen

208

people do it on TV. We can leave a note behind so no one will worry much."

The children quietly left the house and headed for the highway that led out of town.

After a few minutes, a car honked and stopped at the side of the road. It was Mother and Father!

"What are you children doing?" Mother asked.

"We're running away because Daddy doesn't like us anymore," said Joy.

"That's right," said Johnny, looking at Father. "Instead of spending the day with us, you went to play golf with a friend."

209

Let's Rehearse a Bible Verse

Children are a gift from the Lord.
Psalm 127:3

The children saw a tear in Father's eye.

"Kids, I'm sorry you feel this way," he said. "I love you all so much. Johnny must have overheard my conversation with Chris Leavitt. I arranged to buy five tickets from him for the circus today. I just picked them up. It was to be a surprise."

No one had anything to say for a few moments.

"I'm sorry I talked the girls into leaving home, Dad," Johnny finally said.

"So am I," said Father.

"You disappointed your mother and me, and you disappointed God. Let's go home now and discuss how foolish and dangerous running away from home is. . . ."

Father paused before going on. He could see the unasked question in the children's eyes.

"Then we'll go have fun together at the circus."

The children all gave Father a hug, and the Kenton family headed for home.

Check Your Head for What You've Read

1. Did Johnny really have a good reason for thinking Father didn't care about the children?
2. What did Johnny *think* he heard when he overheard part of Father's phone conversation?
3. Why was it wrong for the children to run away from home?

A Look Inside God's Special Book

Do you ever feel like you're not very important? Most of us do at times. But we shouldn't. One day some people brought their children to Jesus so they could touch Him and be blessed by Him. But Jesus' followers told these people to stop bothering Jesus by bringing their children to Him. They said He was too busy to use His time that way. How do you think Jesus felt about this when He found out?

Jesus said, "Let the little children come to me. Don't stop them, because the kingdom of heaven belongs to people who are like these children." Jesus received the children, put His hands on them, and prayed for each one. No one had any more doubts about how important children are to God!

Find this story in Matthew 19, Mark 10, and Luke 18.

When You Pray, Day by Day
Ask God:
• to help you learn not to jump to wrong
conclusions about things people say
• to show you *good* ways to share your concerns and
questions with your parents and other adults.
Thank God for your parents, who love you very
much—even when you aren't sure they do.

Something Fun for Everyone
At some time or other, nearly every child thinks about running away from home.
This may be caused by trouble with a brother or sister, problems at school, conflict
with parents, or any number of other things.

Have a family meeting to discuss the issue of running away. Because this is
a very serious thing to talk about, you will need to find some ways to lighten up
the discussion. Start by making a big bowl of popcorn! Pour glasses of cold juice or
soda, and gather around the dining-room table. (Or have your meeting outside
where you can enjoy the spring sunshine!)

When your family is together, have a family prayer, then discuss topics such as
these:
• alternatives to running away
• good ways to communicate problems and concerns, and to resolve differences
• God's will as it relates to children who want to run away from home (removing
themselves from the protective care of their parents)
• strangers and their possible bad intentions
• other safety factors (the presence and dangers of motor vehicles, animals, insects, bad
weather, and disease)
• God's plan for families and family love.

Something to think about: No problem is so big that you need to run away. Talk
with your parents about the problem . . . and talk with God.

He's Not What I Had in Mind

Dealing with disapointment

Elaina could hardly contain her excitement when she heard a car drive up outside. She ran out to meet her father.

"Did you get the kitten?" she asked.

"It's right here," said Father with a smile as he lifted a box with a handle on top from the seat beside him.

Elaina's parents had decided she was old enough to have a pet of her own. Father had called the pet store and found out they had just one kitten left. So he arranged to go buy it the next day, on his way home from work.

"What color is it, Daddy? Is it orange like I hoped it would be?" asked Elaina as Father carried the box into the house.

213

"No, it's not orange," said father. "It's black with white markings on its chest and feet."

"Oh," said Elaina, looking disappointed. Then she brightened when she said, "I'll bet it's a sweet little girl kitty like I wanted, though. . . ."

"I'm sorry, Elaina," he answered. "It's a male."

"Well, maybe he will curl up on my lap and cuddle, and let me dress him in baby clothes like Aria's girl kitty does. I sure hope so."

Once they were inside the house, the whole family gathered around as Father carefully opened the box. Out sprang a little scruffy-haired, long-tailed kitten with the biggest feet and ears any of them had ever seen!

"It looks like he went through the spin cycle of the washing machine!" said Johnny, laughing.

"He is kind of *different*-looking," added Mother.

"What an ugly cat!" said Joy in her usual no-nonsense way.

Elaina was working hard to hold back tears. She picked up the kitten, but he squirmed free and started running around the house like he was trying to get away from a fire. This was the way the kitten liked to play.

"He . . . he's not the kind of kitty I wanted at all!" said Elaina. "Please take him back to the pet store, Daddy."

At bedtime, Mother talked with Elaina about the kitten.

"Honey, I'm sorry he isn't what you were expecting," she said, "but sometimes we can't have exactly what we want. What if mommies and daddies decided they didn't want to keep their *children* because they didn't like the way they looked or acted? Or what if God did that when we disappoint *Him?*"

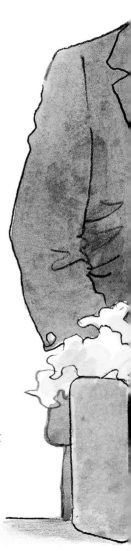

214

Elaina looked thoughtful for a moment. Just then the kitten came into the bedroom and jumped on her bed.

> ### Let's Rehearse a Bible Verse
> We know that in everything God works for the good of those who love him.
> Romans 8:28

It curled up next to her, closed its eyes, and began to make a loud rumbling sound.

"He's purring, Mommy!" said Elaina with a huge smile. The kitten opened one eye and looked at Elaina, then closed it again. It was as if he had wanted to be sure she would make a good owner—and she had passed the test.

"I want to keep him, Mommy. I love my new kitty!"

Mother nodded her head and smiled.

215

Check Your Head for What You've Read

1. What kind of kitten was Elaina hoping her new pet would turn out to be?
2. Why didn't Elaina like her new kitten at first?
3. What did her mother say that helped Elaina decide she wanted to keep the kitten?

A Look Inside God's Special Book

Moses' mother may have been very disappointed when he was born. The wicked king of the Egyptian people had made a law that said all boy babies born to Hebrew mothers would be thrown into the Nile River and killed. Moses' mother didn't want her baby to die!

God didn't want Moses to die either. When Moses was three months old, his mother put him in a basket that had been sealed with tar—so that it would float—and placed it at the edge of the Nile River. The king's daughter found the baby there and decided to raise Moses as her own son. Moses grew to be a great leader of the Hebrew people—right under the bad king's nose!

Find this story in Exodus 1–2.

When You Pray, Day by Day
Ask God:

• to show you the good things behind the
disappointments of life

• to help you love the hard-to-love creatures (and
people) that are part of God's good creation.

Thank God for the good He can bring about, even
at times when you can't see anything good at all.

Something Fun for Everyone

Isn't the story of how God kept Baby Moses alive
amazing? It's been a favorite Bible story of children
for centuries!

Make a baby Moses in a basket. To help you remember how God changed
this situation from one of tragedy to joy, make a basket and a tiny replica of baby
Moses out of clay that you can make yourself. Here's how to make the clay.

INGREDIENTS

3 cups flour	1 cup water
1 cup salt	1 teaspoon lemon juice
3/4 cup white glue	

Mix together the above ingredients in a large bowl. Roll part of your clay out into
a "rope," and begin forming a basket that looks like the one pictured on this page.
(*Hint*: Don't make it too big—a basket three or four inches long is about right.)
Make a handle for the basket by threading a pipe cleaner through the sides, as
shown. Next, mold a baby Moses out of the clay. Let these objects dry overnight
and paint them. Then put Moses in the basket.

Note: You probably will have clay left over. If you put it in a plastic bag, the clay
will remain pliable for several weeks. You can make more figures anytime!

217

Does God Care About My Kitty?

Growing in faith

The Kenton children quickly grew to love Elaina's funny-looking kitten.

"Look what your crazy kitten is doing now!" said Johnny. The kitten was lying upside down against the couch with his hind feet in the air, kicking furiously at a fuzzy ball. He looked like he was standing on his head!

Johnny started calling the kitten Tiberius (the name of an ancient Roman warlord) because he liked to playfully fight with Tommy, the Kentons' huge gray-striped cat. The name stuck.

"Oh Tiberius, you're *goofy*," said Elaina as she tickled the tummy of the upside-down kitten. Tiberius took a playful swat at her finger.

As Mother and Father tucked the children into bed and prayed with them that night, Tiberius jumped onto Elaina's bed—as he did every night—and curled up to go to sleep. Elaina scratched him between the ears and he began to purr.

Elaina loved these quiet moments with her kitten, which seemed to happen only at bedtime.

218

When Elaina woke up the next morning, her kitten was still sleeping. She reached over to pet him and noticed that he felt feverish. She tried to wake the kitten, but the most he would do was open his eyelids halfway, then go back to sleep.

"Mommy, I don't think Tiberius feels good," said Elaina at breakfast.

"What makes you think so, honey?"

"Well, he feels kind of hot, and he won't wake up and play," she answered.

After breakfast, Mother and the children went in to check on Tiberius.

"You're right, Elaina," said Mother. "Tiberius isn't well. I'll ask your father to take him to the vet on the way to work this morning."

Let's Rehearse a Bible Verse

Lord, you have made many things. With your wisdom you made them all . . .
All things depend on you.

Psalm 104:24, 27

"You've got a very sick kitten here, Mr. Kenton," said the veterinarian to Father. "I'll give him some medication, but I don't know if we can save him. He's still so young and small. . . ."

Father stopped at the veterinarian's office on the way home from work to see how Tiberius was doing. There had been no improvement.

"Kids," said Father when he got home, "the vet said Tiberius might die. We need to pray very hard that God will take care of him."

The girls began to cry.

"Daddy?" said Elaina. "D-do you really think God will help my kitty? I don't know if He cares much about cats."

"God loves your kitten," answered Father. "The Bible says God even knows when a little bird falls out of the sky. God cares about Tiberius—and He cares deeply about *you.*"

Father, Mother, and the children prayed for their kitten. The next morning, Mother called the vet.

"I've got some news, Mrs. Kenton," said the vet. "Tiberius is recovering. He's going to be just fine."

Together the Kentons gave thanks to God for His goodness. And Elaina's eyes were wet again—this time from crying tears of happiness.

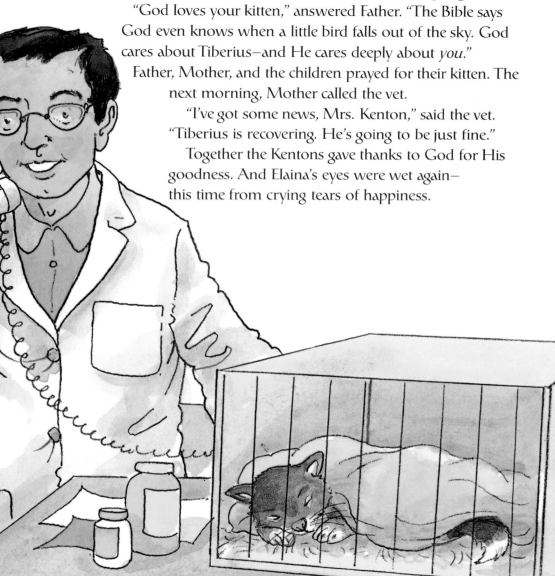

221

Check Your Head for What You've Read

1. How did Elaina know her kitten was not well?
2. What did Father tell Elaina when she asked if God cared about Tiberius?
3. What did the Kenton family do when they found out Elaina's kitten was going to be OK?

A Look Inside God's Special Book

Have you ever wondered how God feels about our pets? Does He love them like we do? The Bible tells us that God made the world and all of creation in just six days. During the first five days he made day and night, the sky and air, rivers and seas, land, plants and trees, the sun, moon and stars, and birds and fish. He made just about *everything* during those five days.

On the sixth day, God said, "Let the earth be filled with animals. And let each produce more of its own kind. Let there be tame animals and small crawling animals and wild animals. And let each produce more of its kind." Then God created man. He made man and the animals on the *same day*, then said that all He had made was "very good."

Read more about this story in Genesis 1.

When You Pray, Day by Day
Ask God:

• to give you an assurance that He loves all of His creatures—even your family pets

• to give you the faith to believe that God hears and answers your prayers.

Thank God for the wonderful creation that you not only can appreciate, but are *part* of.

Something Fun for Everyone

When God created people, He told them they would rule over the animal kingdom. That was a great honor and a *big* responsibility.

Make this Respect-a-Pet Week. A good way to be responsible managers of God's creation right at home is to review some basic pet-care guidelines. (Copy this list and tape it to a wall or refrigerator.)

• Make sure your pet always has plenty of food and water.
• Give your pet as much exercise as it needs.
• Be certain your pet receives all the shots and vitamins it should have (see your veterinarian for a list).
• If your pet is sick, have it seen by a veterinarian.
• Be sure your pet is safe from young children, traffic, other animals, harsh weather, and objects that could cause injury (such as tin cans and broken glass).
• Don't ever leave a pet in a car with the windows rolled up on a warm, sunny day.
• If you have a puppy, be sure to give it chew toys or rawhide chews for teething (and keep your shoes put away and out of reach!).
• So that your pet can be returned to you if it wanders off, license it (if appropriate).
• If your pet enjoys it, play with it often!

Johnny Has the Ball
Patience

"Dad, I'm worried," Johnny said on the way to his first soccer game of the season.

"What's bothering you, son?" Father asked.

"I haven't done very well in practice," he answered.

"Just do your best today, Johnny," said Father. "The main purpose of junior soccer league is to have fun."

The other team, the Buffaloes, had first possession of the ball. Passing the ball from player to player with ease, the Buffaloes sped down the field. One of the biggest players on the team smashed the ball into the corner of the net with the hardest kick Johnny had ever seen. The Buffaloes had scored the first goal.

The Wildcats strengthened their defense after that. But they were having difficulty moving the ball down the field on offense. Every time they had possession of the ball, someone on the other team quickly took it away.

Suddenly the Wildcats had a scoring opportunity: With only one minute left in the first half, Caleb Smith intercepted a

224

225

pass and began dribbling the ball toward the goal.

Let's Rehearse a Bible Verse

Be joyful because you have hope.
Be patient when trouble comes.
Pray at all times.
Romans 12:12

The goalkeeper rushed out to block Caleb, and Caleb swiftly passed the ball to Johnny, who would have a wide-open shot at the goal. Johnny stopped the ball and made a mighty kick. The ball went off the side of his foot and bounced out of play, leaving the Wildcats without a goal.

Both teams did well in the second half. The Buffaloes scored twice and the Wildcats three times, so the scores were equal. Suddenly, Caleb again broke away with the ball and began moving quickly toward the goal. Johnny hurried after him.

This time Johnny was ready when Caleb kicked the ball to him. But the ball hit a bump on the rough field and rose off the ground; Johnny swatted the ball to the ground with his hand.

The referee's whistle sounded shrilly—Johnny had committed a foul, turning the ball over to the Buffaloes. The Wildcats lost the game in overtime.

"I'm finished with soccer," Johnny said on the way home from the game. "Everybody is better than I am."

"It's the first game of the season," Father reminded him. "Give yourself a chance to improve."

"But I was the only one on the team who messed up each time I had the ball," Johnny argued.

"Johnny, what if God were as quick to give up on us as we are to give up on ourselves? What if He said, 'Johnny Kenton sinned today. I will have nothing more to do with him!' But

God doesn't do that. He forgives us and helps us to become stronger and wiser—more like *Him.*"

"Yeah, but this is soccer, Dad. . . ."

"That's true, but patience is a lifestyle, Johnny," answered Father. "Paul said in Romans 12, 'Be patient when trouble comes.' Paul wasn't talking about salvation. He was talking about *life.* . . . Why don't you give soccer another try?"

Johnny stared out the window of the car for a full minute. "OK, Dad. I . . . I guess I'll give it a little more time."

227

Check Your Head for What You've Read

1. Why was Johnny worried before his first soccer game of the season?

2. What did Johnny want to do after he had failed to score any goals in the game? Why?

3. How did Father convince Johnny to continue playing soccer, at least for a while?

A Look Inside God's Special Book

God's timing sometimes isn't what we want it to be. God told Abraham he would have a son. "And your descendants will be too many to count," God said. But many years later, Abraham's wife, Sarah, still hadn't given birth to the promised son. Sarah wanted her servant girl, Hagar, to have a baby, hoping that it might be a son for Abraham.

Hagar became pregnant and gave birth to a son, but not the son God had promised. The promised child was to be Abraham and *Sarah's* son, not Abraham and Hagar's. But Abraham remained faithful, and God did eventually give him and Sarah a son—when Abraham was one hundred years old and Sarah was ninety!

Read more about this story in Genesis 15–21.

When You Pray, Day by Day
Ask God:
• to give you the patience to work through problems
• to give you the desire to become more like Jesus.
Thank God for the hope we have because we know He hears our prayers and cares about us.

Something Fun for Everyone
Being patient often means having to wait for something. You may need to wait until tomorrow, next week, or even *years* from now–rather than have what you want today.

Make a Patience Poster. Have you ever had to wait for something a long, long time? Waiting can be difficult, but good things often don't happen right away.

At the top of a sheet of poster board or construction paper, write the words "Worth the Wait" with a marker. Across the bottom, write out the words of 2 Timothy 2:24: "And a servant of the Lord must not quarrel but must be kind to everyone, a good teacher, and patient."

Next, think about things that grow–such as flowers, animals, and people. Draw a picture of the stages something must go through before it shows a particular result. For example, you could show a fruit tree that has buds, then flowers, then the yummy fruit that you can pick and eat. Or draw a picture of a tadpole that eventually grows legs, then finally becomes a frog that you can catch.

Display your poster in your bedroom. When you look at it, remember to ask God for the patience to wait until you become the person that He wants you to be. It *will* be worth the wait!

Give It Your Best Shot!
Trusting God

"You've looked good in practice this week, guys, so let's win this game!" said coach Kelleher. It was the Wildcats' second soccer game of the season.

Johnny had spent the week practicing his footwork. He and Champion had even practiced kicking the ball at home after their daily team practices.

Please help me do my best today, Lord, Johnny silently prayed as he waited for Caleb Smith to kick off, starting the game.

The Wildcats' opponents, the Timber Wolves, were aggressive. Twice early in the first half, the referee blew his whistle because one of the Timber Wolves had intentionally pushed or tripped one of Johnny's teammates. The Wildcats were awarded free kicks each time, but they were not able to score.

Using skillful footwork, Caleb Smith managed to take the ball away from one of the Timber Wolves. Within a few moments he was in scoring position, near the Timber Wolves' goal. But before Caleb could score, a defending player kicked

230

231

Caleb in the shin with all of his might. Caleb fell to the ground and grabbed his injured leg. Coach Kelleher and Champion helped Caleb off the field; he would not be able to return that day.

The coach asked Johnny to take the penalty kick for Caleb.

The ball was placed on the ground. *I won't let you and the team down, Caleb,* Johnny thought. His foot struck the ball solidly, it bounced along the ground—but it went to the right of the goal.

When Johnny returned to the sidelines at halftime, there was still no score.

"Nice kick, Johnny," said Caleb, who sat on the bench, an ice pack on his swollen shin. "You'll get the next one," he added.

"Thanks, Caleb, but it should have been an easy goal."

"You're getting better all the time, Johnny. You guys can win this game."

The second half went much like the first. The other team committed lots of fouls, and neither team could score. The game was nearly over, and Johnny was worried.

A Timber Wolves player kicked the ball out of play, and one of Johnny's teammates tossed the ball in to Johnny. Johnny kicked the ball hard and scampered after it. The goal was just ahead. Seeing that the goalkeeper was prepared to block his kick, Johnny passed the ball to Champion. Champion kicked it right back.

Just like Caleb's kick the week before, the ball lifted off the ground as it neared Johnny. *Not again!* Johnny groaned inwardly. But instead of hitting the ball with his hand, Johnny smacked it with his head—right into the net. He had scored!

Let's Rehearse a Bible Verse

Faith means being sure of the things we hope for. And faith means knowing that something is real even if we do not see it.

Hebrews 11:1

Time ran out and the game was over.

Champion slapped Johnny on the back. "Nice work, Johnny!" he said. "You just won the game!"

Johnny smiled back. Then he closed his eyes and bowed his head for a silent prayer. *Thank you, Lord, for helping me do my best.*

Check Your Head for What You've Read

1. What did Johnny pray before the soccer game began?

2. What did Johnny do to help his team win?

3. Do you think God answered Johnny's first prayer? Why do you think so?

A Look Inside God's Special Book

It's always a good idea to trust God to help you. One day a woman went to a place where Jesus was talking to some people. This woman had a very serious problem—she'd been bleeding for twelve years, and her condition was getting worse. But she believed Jesus could heal her. So she'd gone to where He was speaking.

There were many people gathered to hear Jesus, but the sick woman thought, "*If I can even touch his coat, that will be enough to heal me.*" When she did touch His coat, power flowed from Jesus to the woman. Without seeing her do it, Jesus knew someone of great faith had touched Him. The woman was healed instantly! "Dear woman," Jesus said, "you are made well because you believed. Go in peace. You will have no more suffering."

Find this story in Mark 5 and Luke 8.

When You Pray, Day by Day

Ask God:

• to make you confident that He will help you when you ask Him for help
• to teach you not to be hard on yourself when you can't do things as well as you like.

Thank God for His gift of faith that allows us to believe His promises and have hope for the future.

Something Fun for Everyone

Have you ever thought about how much faith it takes to be a farmer? The farmer plants a little seed in the ground and believes a plant will grow. That takes faith.

Grow a Garden of Faith.

To do this, you will need a clear plastic drink cup, three solid-color paper towels (not white if possible—colored towels show the roots of young plants better), and four bean seeds.

Wad up the paper towels and stuff them into the cup. Push the bean seeds down along the inside of the cup, between the cup and the towels. (They should be about halfway down the side, and spaced evenly around the cup.) Apply enough water to wet the towels, but not enough to form puddles on the bottom of the cup.

Place your garden on a sunny windowsill, and sprinkle it with water as often as needed. Watch the seeds sprout and grow!

As your plants grow, let your faith in God grow too—the miracle of life would never happen if God didn't make it happen!

Sunday Snafu
Preparing our hearts to worship God

"Rise and shine, girls," said Mother cheerfully as she opened the curtains in the girls' room. "It's time to get ready for Sunday school."

"Can't we do something else today, Mommy?" grumbled Elaina. "Trina's family is going to the zoo. Why don't *we* do something like that?"

"Because on Sundays we go to church to learn about God and to show Him that we love Him," explained Mother.

Mother went down the hall to Johnny's room.

"Good morning, Johnny!" she said. "It's time to get ready for church."

"Oh n-o-o-o," he moaned. "It can't be time to get up already!" Johnny pressed his face into his pillow.

"Let's get moving, Johnny," Mother said. "We don't want to be late."

Let's Rehearse a Bible Verse

Praise the Lord for the glory of his name.
Worship the Lord because he is holy.

Psalm 29:2

A few minutes later, Mother checked on the children's progress. Elaina and Joy were arguing over who was going to wear the pink headband, and Johnny was still in bed. None of the children had even *started* to get ready.

Mother again told each of them to get dressed.

"Breakfast is ready," called out Father. He peeked into the girls' room.

Joy, why aren't you getting dressed?" he asked. She was sitting in a corner of the room playing with her doll. "Elaina! You're not dressed either!"

"I don't have anything nice to wear," she answered. She had pulled three pretty dresses down from the closet and laid them on the floor in front of her.

When Father checked on Johnny, he found him half-dressed and lying on his bed looking at baseball cards. Father told him that breakfast was getting cold.

The family finally gathered at the kitchen table for breakfast. The girls resumed their squabble.

"I need to wear the pink headband because it goes better with my dress," said Elaina.

"It does *not*," Joy answered. "I had it first."

"Girls, please stop arguing and eat," said Father. "Uh-oh, look what time it is . . . we're going to be late! Come on, kids, let's go to the car."

238

"We can't go yet!" said Johnny. "I haven't had a chance to comb my hair."

"Children," said Mother, "we're already late, but we need to talk. You haven't cooperated with us this morning. Now we're late. Is this any way to show God we love Him?"

The children slowly shook their heads.

"I don't think so either," said Mother.

"What do you think we should do about this?" Father asked the children.

Johnny, Joy, and Elaina looked back and forth at each other, but no one answered.

"Well, I think we need to ask God to forgive us," said Father. "And I think we need to ask Jesus to help us leave here with an attitude of love and praise for Him in our hearts. What do you think?"

The children nodded their heads, and the family prayed.

Check Your Head for What You've Read

1. In what ways were the Kenton children not cooperating with their parents?

2. Did their behavior show honor for the children's parents? Did it honor God?

3. What did Father think the family needed to do before they left for Sunday school? Why?

A Look Inside God's Special Book

It's important to worship God with all your heart. Long ago, the king of Babylon had a tall gold statue built. The king told the people of the vast empire of Babylon that they would have to bow down and worship the statue when they heard special music play.

What was the penalty for failing to obey the king's new law? Those who failed to obey would be thrown into a blazing-hot furnace and killed!

Shadrach, Meshach, and Abednego were three young men who loved God. They refused to bow down when the music played. They said they would rather die than worship a false God. The king was furious. He ordered the men to be thrown into the furnace. But a strange thing happened. God sent an angel to them to protect them, and they weren't hurt at all!

Find this story in Daniel 3.

When You Pray, Day by Day

Ask God:

• to show you how to honor Him and your parents with your behavior

• to help you desire to worship God with a heart full of praise and love.

Thank God for being able to worship Him and for being able to openly proclaim your love for Him.

Something Fun for Everyone

It's never fun around the house when people are arguing and unhappy about everything. This is an especially bad way to start off Sundays!

Sketch a Sunday Worship Strategy. A *good* way to prepare for Sunday worship is to organize ahead of time. Because every family is different, help design a worship strategy that works for *your* family. Write these down and look at them often. You may want to include some of these ideas:

On Saturday night:

• Lay out all the clothes and accessories you will need for Sunday morning.
• Put your Bible and any Sunday school materials you need where they can be easily seen.
• Go to bed early.
• Pray at bedtime that you can help everything go smoothly in the morning when you get up.

On Sunday morning:

• Get up promptly.
• Get dressed, fix your hair, and make a deliberate effort not to argue with brothers, sisters, or your parents.
• Go to the table when you are called to breakfast, and eat what has been prepared—without complaining.
• On the way to church, think about reasons you love God!

SUMMER

June

July

August

Unwanted Award

Get even or show mercy?

"Hi, Eli," said Elaina. She had come to Eli's house to take him for a walk. Because Eli was in a wheelchair, this was something he couldn't do on his own.

"G-good m-morning, Elaina," he answered.

"Aren't you glad school is out?" she asked her friend.

"Y-yes . . . I am," he answered. "I d-didn't like it m-m-much." The illness that kept Eli in a wheelchair also made speaking difficult for him.

"But you did well in school," she said. "You're a good student. Better than most, anyway. I heard that Jeremy Brown has to go to summer school—or else be in first grade again next fall."

"G-good!" said Eli as his head wobbled back and forth. I-I hope he *is* in f-first g-grade again!"

Elaina knew why Eli felt this way. Jeremy had been in Eli and Elaina's class at school. He had been cruel to Eli all year long, making fun of Eli's physical problems.

"I know Jeremy wasn't nice to you, Eli," said Elaina. "But you shouldn't be glad he's in trouble at school."

244

"B-but I *am* glad!" said Eli. "He . . . he c-called me a d-dummy. *He's* really the d-d-dummy! I'd like h-him to feel bad like I always d-did."

Elaina was surprised at Eli's anger.

"I'm going t-to get C-Caleb to help me m-make Jeremy an award—the 'Class D-Dummy' award I'll call it!" Caleb was Eli's older brother.

Elaina pushed Eli's wheelchair under the shade of a big maple tree in the park. She sat down on a bench under the tree.

"Mommy says people who make fun of other people

245

usually feel bad about themselves," said Elaina. "She says people like Jeremy need our help, Eli. If we can help them feel better about themselves, sometimes they'll be kinder to other people."

"It's h-hard to be nice to p-people who act like they h-hate you," he answered.

"Yes it is," Elaina agreed. "But Mommy and Daddy always say that Jesus *wants* us to do it. He wants us to do good things to people who do bad things to us."

Eli looked away from Elaina. "I w-wasn't really going t-to send Jeremy a d-dummy award," said Eli. "I just s-said that because he m-makes me so *mad*."

Elaina smiled and nodded at her friend.

"I'd like to d-do what J-Jesus wants me to do," he said. "C-can you h-help me think of some . . . s-something nice to do for Jeremy?"

"That's a great idea!" she answered. "Let's just sit here for a while and see what we can think of."

Eli gave Elaina a happy, wobbly grin.

Let's Rehearse a Bible Verse

Forget about the wrong things people do to you. You must not try to get even. Love your neighbor as you love yourself.

Leviticus 19:18

Check Your Head for What You've Read

1. Why was Eli glad to find out that Jeremy Brown would be held back in the first grade if he didn't go to summer school?
2. What did Eli want to do to Jeremy at first?
3. What reason did Elaina give for not wanting Eli to send Jeremy a "Class Dummy" award?

A Look Inside God's Special Book

It's easy to like people who are kind to you. But Jesus taught that there is much more to being kind than this. One day when He was teaching, Jesus said: "You have heard that it was said, 'Love your neighbor and hate your enemies.' But I tell you, love your enemies. Pray for those who hurt you."

Jesus went on to say that God lets the sun shine on both good people and bad people. And He sends refreshing rain to everyone, too. He said, "If you are nice only to your friends, then you are no better than other people." Jesus went on to promise that people who love those who hate them will be rewarded in heaven.

Find this story in Matthew 5:43–48. Read a related story–the story of Joseph–in Genesis 37–45.

When You Pray, Day by Day
Ask God:
• to help you show mercy to those who hurt you or are unkind to you in some other way
• to show you how to have Jesus' love for people who do bad things to you.
Thank God for His promise of a heavenly reward for sharing His love with others.

Something Fun for Everyone
Whether you're trying to be merciful to someone who has done something bad to you or you just want to do something kind for a friend or someone you know, doing things for others will do *your* heart a lot of good.

Compile a summer jobs list. Begin looking for things you might do for others and write them down. Start at home. Then look around at the needs of people in your neighborhood (and try not to forget the elderly lady next door who complains that your ball always winds up in her yard). If you need help getting started, here is a short list of jobs you might do.

• Clean the garage.
• Wash the car.
• Weed and hoe the garden or do yard work.
• Water plants and trees in the yard.
• Offer to fold laundry.
• Take out the garbage.
• Offer to collect the mail for someone who is going on vacation.
• Walk your neighbors' dog for them, or offer to take care of their pets while they're on vacation.
• If you deliver newspapers, consider putting newspapers for elderly people or people with handicaps on the porch of the house rather than on the sidewalk or in a delivery tube at the street.
Once you have a list, start working your way through it! Helping others will make you feel good, and it usually brings out the best in those we help, too.

249

Entering Dangerous Territory
Being kind to those who don't like you

"Whew—it's really *hot!*" said Elaina as she pushed her friend Eli along the sidewalk.

"Y-you can say th-*that* again," said Eli. "M-maybe we shouldn't g-go today."

Eli and Elaina had decided to pay a friendly visit to Jeremy Brown, who had not been friendly to Eli.

"Sure we should go," said Elaina. "Even though Jeremy hasn't been friendly to you, we promised each other we would be kind to him—because that's what Jesus wants us to do. Remember?"

"I r-remember," he answered. "I'm j-just a little afraid to s-see him."

They walked a few more blocks until they came to a mobile home park at the edge of town.

"We're looking for number 23," said Elaina. Finally, they found the address they were looking for. It was an old, tan-colored mobile home. Elaina knocked on the door.

"Hello," said Jeremy's mother as she opened the door. Elaina explained that they had come to see Jeremy.

"Come around to the back," his mother said. Turning to Eli, she said, "I think we can get your wheelchair through our sliding patio door."

Elaina and Eli followed her to the back door. Once inside, they saw Jeremy sitting at the dining-room table. He was doing homework.

251

"Hi, Jeremy," said Elaina. Surprised, Jeremy turned around and faced his visitors.

"Why are *you* here?" he asked suspiciously.

"W-we just came to v-visit," answered Eli.

"With me, the class dunce?" asked Jeremy.

"Don't feel bad about being in summer school, Jeremy," said Elaina. "It doesn't mean you're dumb—it just means you need to do some more work."

"Yeah, maybe so," said Jeremy. "I goofed off during the year and got so far behind that I don't know if I can catch up. . . ."

"W-would you like h-help?" asked Eli. "I'm a p-pretty good st-student, and I d-don't have much to do this s-summer. . . ."

"*You* would help *me?*" asked Jeremy. He had a surprised look on his face.

"S-sure," he answered. "I'd really l-like to. On one c-condition."

"Uh . . . what's that?" asked Jeremy, with suspicion again in his voice.

"That w-we can be *f-friends.*"

"I . . . I don't know," Jeremy answered. Then he brightened. "You'd really like to be my friend?"

Eli gave his head a wobbly nod.

Let's Rehearse a Bible Verse

Where God's love is, there is no fear,
because God's perfect love takes away fear.

1 John 4:18

Jeremy smiled. "I'd *like* to be your friend, Eli," he said. "And yours too, Elaina."

After Elaina and Eli left, Jeremy's mother came back into the room from the kitchen.

"Your friends seem very nice, Jeremy," she said.

"Yes, Mom, they are," he said.

I wonder why they decided to come here today? Jeremy asked himself. *Maybe I'll find out someday.*

253

Check Your Head for What You've Read

1. Why did Elaina and Eli visit Jeremy Brown?
2. Was Eli afraid to see Jeremy at first?
3. Why do you think Jeremy was surprised when Eli asked him if they could be friends?
4. Was Jesus honored by what Eli and Elaina did?

A Look Inside God's Special Book

Jesus often used stories to teach people things they needed to know. One day, Jesus told some people the kingdom of God is like a mustard seed.

"That seed is the smallest of all seeds," He said. "But when it grows, it is one of the largest garden plants. It becomes a tree, big enough for the wild birds to come and make nests in its branches."

Jesus was saying that God's kingdom can start small, but it will grow much larger as Jesus' followers share the Good News about His love. Here's how this works: One person tells someone else what Jesus has done in his life. When this second person believes in Jesus and sees what Jesus can do in his life, then he, like his friend, tells others. Then *those* people share with still others. That's how the kingdom of God grows!

Read this story in Matthew 13 and Mark 4.

When You Pray, Day by Day
Ask God:
• to help you learn how to take risks for God
• to show you good ways to share God's love with other people.

Thank God that His perfect love can take away your fears.

Something Fun for Everyone

Jesus said the kingdom of God is like a mustard seed—it starts small but grows very big in time. Have you ever wondered just how small a mustard seed really is? The following activity will *show* you. And you'll have a lot of fun, too!

Make a seed picture. To do this, you will need several different kinds of seeds—such as rice, beans, barley, split peas, pumpkin, and mustard seeds (available in the spices section of the grocery store). Then follow these steps:

1. Draw a simple design on a piece of tag board (or sturdy cardboard). The size of the board can vary, but don't make it too large—a 12- by 12-inch square would work well.

2. Plan where each kind of seed will go.

3. Working with one kind of seed at a time, brush a thick coat of white glue where that type of seed will go, and put the seeds in place.

4. After all areas of your seed picture are filled in with seeds, let the picture dry.

When the picture is dry, compare the mustard seed to the other seeds you used. It's far smaller than the others, but it will grow into a bigger plant than any of them! So don't think anything you can do for God's kingdom is too small!

Life in the Blast Lane
Sticking with your convictions

"Oh man, are we ever gonna have fun!" said Champion as he and Johnny helped Father unload the car. Johnny grinned back at his friend.

The Kentons were taking their vacation at the ocean this year. For the next three weeks they would be staying in a cabin on the beach. Champion had come too.

Everyone spent the next couple of days getting settled into a vacation routine. They played in the water, made sand castles, did some fishing off the pier—and just plain had fun.

"What do you say we do a little exploring today?" suggested Johnny one morning.

"Good idea," said Champion. "Let's go!"

After discussing with Mother and Father exactly where they were headed and when they would return, Johnny and Champion set off walking up the beach. Soon they came upon some teenagers playing volleyball. They stopped to watch.

"Do you think they'd let us play?" whispered Champion. Before Johnny could answer, a boy came over to them.

"We're a couple of people short today," he began.

"Would you kids like to join us?"

Johnny and Champion couldn't believe their luck!

"This is really *living*," said Champion to Johnny after he smacked the ball over the net. "I wish we could stay here all summer!"

257

After completing a game, they stopped for a break.

"Want something to drink?" said a tall blonde boy wearing the wildest swim trunks Johnny and Champion had ever seen.

"You bet we do!" said Champion.

The boy rummaged around in the ice chest for a minute. He came back with two cold cans of beverage, dripping wet from the ice. Johnny couldn't believe his eyes–they were cans of beer!

"This is all we've got left, guys," the tall boy was saying. "Think you're man enough?"

Champion slowly reached out and took one of the cans.

"No, Champion!" Johnny said. "You can't!"

"I'll just have a few sips," Champion whispered to his friend.

"It wouldn't be right," said Johnny. "Let's go."

Champion handed the can back to the boy, and he and Johnny left. Neither of the boys spoke until their cabin was in sight.

"I know your parents wouldn't like you drinking beer, Champion," said Johnny finally. "Neither would mine. And you promised your parents you'd obey my family's rules on this trip."

"I just didn't want to seem like a little kid," he finally answered. "And . . . and I guess I figured no one would need to know."

"*God* would know," said Johnny.

Champion stared down at his feet as they walked. "Yeah, you're probably right. . . . I'm sorry, Johnny. Maybe you can show me how God can help me stick to my guns–the way *you* do."

258

Let's Rehearse a Bible Verse

Stay away from the evil things young people love to do.

2 Timothy 2:22

"Sure," answered Johnny. "The Bible is a good place to start. Race you to the cabin to get it?"

"You're on!" said Champion.

259

Check Your Head for What You've Read

1. What did the volleyball player on the beach offer Johnny and Champion to drink? Why did Champion accept it?

2. When Champion said he thought he could get away with a few sips of beer because no one would know, what did Johnny say?

3. Where can we learn how to do what is right?

A Look Inside God's Special Book

Daniel and his three friends, Shadrach, Meshach, and Abednego, were Hebrew captives in the city of Babylon. The king told his servant to give Daniel and his friends food and wine from his own table. But Daniel decided eating the king's food would not be right in God's eyes.

Daniel said, "Please give us this test for ten days: Don't give us anything but vegetables to eat and water to drink. Then after ten days compare us with the other young men who eat the king's food. See for yourself who looks healthier." God honored the men's desire to remain faithful to Him. At the end of the ten days they were healthier than all the men who had eaten the king's food!

Find this story in Daniel 1.

When You Pray, Day by Day
Ask God:

• to help you develop rules for living that honor God and your parents
• to give you the strength and desire to say no to things you shouldn't do.

Thank God that He will help you stick up for what you believe when you ask Him to.

Something Fun for Everyone

Because everyone is tempted to do wrong things, God gave us ways to deal with temptation. Where can we find out how God can help us resist temptation? The *Bible*.

Let's explore the Bible. Read the following questions, then look up the Bible verses in parentheses. If you still need help, the answers are at the bottom of the page.

1. Who was the first person ever to be tempted to do wrong? (*Genesis 3:1–6*)
2. What will the Lord give to us that can help us to make good choices? (*Proverbs 2:6*)
3. What should you do if someone asks you to do something that you believe is wrong? (*Proverbs 4:14*)
4. What is the best thing to do if you know someone who you think might ask you to do something wrong? (*Proverbs 4:15*)
5. If you trust God to help you live right but you are tempted to do wrong, how will He help you? (*1 Corinthians 10:13*)
6. What did Jesus' friend Peter say you should do when you do bad things? (*Acts 3:19*)

ANSWERS: (1) Eve (2) wisdom (3) Don't do what they say. (4) Stay away from that person. (5) He will show you a way to not do what is wrong. (6) Change your heart and life so that God will forgive you.

Emergency on the Beach
God will provide

Mother, Joy, and Elaina were spending the morning at the beach. Father and the boys had gone fishing. "Let's make a sand castle," suggested Elaina.

"I want to make my *own* sand castle," said Joy. "I'll make it the *biggest* one in the whole world."

"I've got an idea," said Elaina. "Let's race and see who can be the first to build a castle *this* high." Elaina was on her knees and held her hand out straight.

"OK," answered Joy.

"Can I play too?" asked a little girl of about Joy's age.

"Sure," answered Elaina. "What's your name?"
"Hannah," she said. "My mommy's over there." The girl pointed to a woman under a beach umbrella nearby.

"Ready, set, *go!*" said Joy, eager to get on with the race. The girls worked quickly. Elaina soon had a solid base for her castle. She made it by filling her bucket with wet sand and carefully turning it upside down, again and again, packing the sand firmly each time.

Joy wasn't worried about neatness. She just wanted to finish her castle *fast!* She used her bucket as a giant scoop, and was making a big mound of sand.

262

Hannah didn't have a bucket—she had only a thin plastic shovel that wasn't strong enough to scoop the wet sand. So she was first scooping sand into a pile with her hands, then shaping and smoothing the sand with the shovel.

Suddenly Hannah screamed. She had cut her wrist on a broken bottle that she had uncovered with her hand as she was digging. It was a deep cut.

"What should we do?" shouted Hannah's mother. "She'll bleed to death!"

Mother took hold of Hannah's little arm and squeezed hard on the jagged cut. But the bleeding wouldn't stop.

Hannah wasn't crying. She was pale, and she just stared ahead in silence.

Let's Rehearse a Bible Verse

Do not worry about anything. But pray and ask God for everything you need. And when you pray, always give thanks.

Philippians 4:6

"Get blankets! She's going into shock!" said Mother. "We need to keep her warm!"

Hannah's mother was crying and screaming for help. A crowd gathered, but no one with medical training was in the crowd.

"Dear God, we need help for this precious child," Mother prayed out loud. "And Lord, we need it *soon*."

Just then a man who had been jogging down the beach with his wife noticed Mother and Hannah.

"Step aside!" he said as he pushed his way through the crowd. "I'm a doctor."

The doctor took over Mother's job and laid Hannah on her back. He sent his wife back to their vacation cabin nearby for medical supplies. He asked her to call an ambulance, too.

The doctor had stopped the bleeding by the time the ambulance arrived. Hannah's mother climbed into the ambulance beside her daughter.

"She's going to be all right," said the doctor to Mother. "Your quick action saved her life."

"*God* saved that little girl's life," said Mother with tears in her eyes. "I was just His helper . . . and so were you."

Check Your Head for What You've Read

1. How did little Hannah become hurt?
2. What did Mother do to try to help Hannah? Do you think Mother's prayer helped?
3. What did Mother say to the doctor when he told her she had saved Hannah's life? What did she mean when she said she was God's "helper"?

A Look Inside God's Special Book

The Lord wants to meet the needs of His people. After Moses led the Israelites out of captivity in Egypt, they said to him, "It would have been better if the Lord had killed us in the land of Egypt. There we had meat to eat. We had all the food we wanted. But you have brought us into this desert. You will starve us to death here."

God told Moses He would send a special kind of bread to the Israelites that they could pick up off the ground each morning. This bread was called *manna*. And each evening, God sent huge flocks of quail to the people for their meat at dinner time. In this way God provided for the Israelites, and they knew it was God who was caring for them.

Find this story in Exodus 16.

When You Pray, Day by Day
Ask God:
• to give you the faith to trust Him to provide for your needs, even during emergencies
• to help you learn how to pray with thanks.
Thank God that He uses people who trust Him, to be His helpers.

Something Fun for Everyone
Will you be taking a family vacation or trip this summer? If you are, make sure you're prepared for emergencies.

Make a family first-aid kit. A travel first-aid kit should contain the items listed below, plus any special items your family may need (such as a bee-sting kit if someone in the family is allergic to bee stings).

• 1 bottle syrup of ipecac
• 1 small container pain reliever (aspirin or non-aspirin type)
• 1 cold pack
• 1 one-inch-wide roll of waterproof tape
• 1 pair scissors, 1 pair tweezers, 1 eye dropper
• 1 bar antiseptic soap
• 1 package adhesive bandages (assorted sizes)
• 1 package butterfly closures
• 1 thermometer
• 1 small penlight with batteries
• 2 triangular bandages
• several 2- by 2-inch sterile dressings in sealed envelopes
• several 4- by 4-inch sterile dressings in sealed envelopes
• 2 fifteen-foot roller bandages, two inches wide
• 1 tube first-aid cream
• 1 first-aid book (call your local Red Cross chapter for titles)

Collect the above items and place them in a waterproof container. (A druggist or clerk can help you locate them in the store.) Take your kit with you and enjoy your trip!

Flag Folly

Patriotism and God

The children were excited. This was a national holiday, and the Kentons and Champion were going into town to see a parade.

"Let's see," said Mother. "Our lunch is packed, and we have fold-up chairs in the car. I think we're ready to go."

When they got to town, the Kentons found everything decorated with banners, streamers, and balloons. And everywhere the children looked, they saw flags proudly flapping in the warm breeze.

267

"It's so pretty!" said Joy as the family set up chairs along the street.

"Wow! Look at that *tall* man!" shouted Elaina.

"He's using stilts," said Father as a man who must have been ten feet tall walked stiffly up the street. He had white whiskers on his chin and was dressed in a colorful costume that included a coat with long tails and pants with broad stripes. On his head he wore a tall hat with a band of stars around it.

"How can he be so tall?" asked Joy.

"It's because he always eats his vegetables," joked Johnny.

Joy had a puzzled look on her face. The others all laughed.

"Stilts are long poles with a footrest sometimes several feet above the ground. They make a person *look* very tall," explained Father. "That man is probably no taller than I am."

Following the man on stilts came a marching band, several colorful floats decorated with paper and flowers, and some shiny convertibles carrying government officials. Champion laughed when a clown with huge feet and a tiny hat squirted water at him from a tiny flower on the lapel of his coat!

Everyone turned and looked up the street when they heard patriotic music being played by a marching band. Suddenly, a man rushed out into the street and unrolled a bundle he was carrying—*it was an American flag!* Then he dumped gasoline on the flag and set it on fire.

"Down with America!" the man shouted as police put handcuffs on him and removed the burning flag from the street.

Let's Rehearse a Bible Verse

No one rules unless God has given him the power to rule.
And no one rules now without that power from God.

Romans 13:1

On the way back to their beach cabin, the family talked about what had happened.

"Daddy, why did that man burn the flag and say what he did?" asked Elaina.

"We are celebrating today because we are free. We're proud of our country," Father answered. "That man isn't proud of this country.

"Our country *isn't* perfect. But it was established by men and women of high principle. Many of our ancestors loved God with all their heart. God has blessed us with freedom and has made our country one of the greatest nations on earth."

"Will this always be a great country, Mr. Kenton?" asked Champion.

"Many people in our country have turned their hearts away from God," Father answered. "Not as many people live by Christian principles now. We need to pray very hard that the United States will return to God. If it doesn't, I don't know how long it will be great. I just don't know. . . ."

They drove the rest of the way to the cabin in silence.

269

Check Your Head for What You've Read

1. As a band played patriotic music, a man ran out into the street. What did he do?

2. Why did the man set the flag on fire? Was it wrong to do this?

3. What did Father say must happen for this country to remain great? How can we help that to happen?

A Look Inside God's Special Book

God's people didn't always have a government made up of men to rule over them. God ruled the people, and He spoke to them through prophets, men God had chosen to tell the people how they should live. But the people weren't satisfied. They wanted to have a king.

God's prophet Samuel told God the people wanted a king. God said, "Listen to whatever the people say to you. They have not rejected you. They have rejected me from being their king." God told Samuel to warn the people that they would not always be happy with their king, and that the king would do exactly what he wanted to do. But they wouldn't listen. So they were given a king. Many kings ruled Israel after that, and some of them were bad.

Find this story in 1 Samuel 8–9.

When You Pray, Day by Day

Ask God:

• to help you love and respect your country

• to turn the hearts of people in your country—and in nations around the world—toward Him.

Thank God for our flag and the freedoms we enjoy, especially the freedom to worship Him.

Something Fun for Everyone

God has blessed this country and made it special. Here are some ways to celebrate our freedom!

• **Read the Declaration of Independence.** As a family, study the document that set us on the road to freedom.

• **Have a bicycle parade.** If your community isn't having a parade, organize one! First, get as many friends together as possible. Fly flags from bikes, tricycles, wagons and scooters, and parade around your neighborhood!

• **Make a flag cake.** Frost a sheet cake with white frosting. Then, using banana and strawberry slices for stripes and blueberries as stars, decorate the cake so that it looks like an American flag. **Hint:** Dip the banana slices in lemon juice to preserve their color. The next step? Eat and celebrate!

A Show to Remember
Obedience

Today the children were going to see an air show—right here at the beach! It would be a good way to end their vacation. Tomorrow they would be going home.

"It's going to be crowded on the beach today, kids," said Father, "so stay near your mother and me. It would be dangerous for any of you to be out of our sight. Do you all understand?"

Each of the children nodded.

"We'll leave as soon as Hannah and her mommy get here," added Mother.

The Kenton family had gotten to know Hannah and her mother well after Hannah received a serious cut on her wrist a week and a half earlier.

Once their guests arrived, the group headed for the beach. They wanted to be close to the water so the children could wade during the air show.

"This is going to be really *cool*," said Johnny, after the towels and blankets were spread out. "Want to throw the Frisbee until the show starts?"

272

"Sure," answered Champion. "Where is it?"

The boys hunted through a canvas bag that held the beach toys, but the Frisbee wasn't there.

"Who used my Frisbee and didn't return it?" asked Johnny.

"Uh-oh," Joy whispered to Hannah. "I used his Frisbee to dig in the sand yesterday. I think I forgot to put it back!"

273

Just then, the air show began. Six jets flying side by side came streaking down the beach. Suddenly they split up and went off in six different directions. It was noisy, but exciting!

"This is *great*," said Father. He dropped his eyes to check on the children. "Hey, where are Joy and Hannah?"

They had sneaked off to hunt for the Frisbee!

"I know it's around *somewhere*," said Joy. "We need to find it fast and get back to Mommy and Daddy. They said we weren't supposed to leave." She and Hannah had been wandering hand-in-hand through the crowd for quite a while by now.

"Which way *is* back?" asked Hannah.

"Don't be goofy!" Joy answered. "Everyone is right over—" She turned around, but saw only hundreds of people she didn't know.

"Let's look for the Frisbee later," suggested Joy. "I think we need to find our mommies right now."

The girls searched for a long, long time. They were afraid. Still holding hands, they finally started running through the crowd. Suddenly, Joy ran right into a man and fell down. She began to cry.

"I c-can't find my *m-mommy*," she sobbed.

"Are you Joy Kenton?" asked the man.

She nodded her head. Joy suddenly noticed that the man was a policeman.

"I thought so," said the policeman. "We've been looking for you two girls for over an hour."

He used a portable radio to let the other

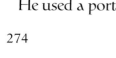

Let's Rehearse a Bible Verse

Children, obey your parents the way the Lord wants.
This is the right thing to do.

Ephesians 6:1

searchers know the girls had been found.
Then he reached down and rumpled the
hair of both girls.

"Come on, you two," he said, "let's go
find your parents."

277

Check Your Head for What You've Read

1. Why did Joy disobey her parents? Was it OK for her to disobey since she was looking for Johnny's Frisbee?
2. Could the girls have been in danger when they wandered off? How?
3. Who finally found the girls?

A Look Inside God's Special Book

God gave Moses the Ten Commandments on the top of Mount Sinai. He told Moses to say to the people, "You must not have any other gods except me. You must not make for yourselves any idols."

The Israelites agreed to honor God by obeying His commandments. Moses left Aaron in charge of the people and went back up Mount Sinai to receive God's Law on a set of stone tablets.

After Moses had been gone for many days, the people said to Aaron, "Moses led us out of Egypt. But we don't know what has happened to him. So make us gods who will lead us."

Aaron unwisely agreed to do what they asked. He made a calf out of gold and the people worshiped it as if it was God! God severely punished the people for this.

Find this story in Exodus 20; 24; and 32.

When You Pray, Day by Day

Ask God:
- to help you obey your parents and God
- to keep you safe if you ever become separated from your parents.

Thank God for giving us rules that protect us and help us live good lives.

Something Fun for Everyone

After you have a fun, safe vacation or outing this summer, do something to preserve the "treasures" you collect (seashells, rocks, feathers, small pieces of wood or driftwood, and so on). Here are some ways to do that.

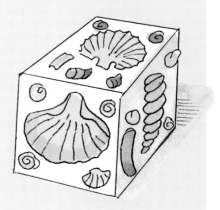

- **Make a necklace.** Thread a string through some of your treasures, making a necklace.
- **Make a "treasure box."** Glue some of your summer treasures (like small rocks and seashells) to a shoe box. Store other special items inside the box.
- **Make wind chimes.** Dangle your collected items from strings that are tied to a wood dowel or a clothes hanger. Let them clatter in the wind.
- **Make a sand-casting.** Place some of your treasures in a 2-inch-deep "mold" you have scooped in the sand. Pour mixed plaster of Paris (available at craft stores) over the things in the mold, and let it set for one hour. Then remove and brush off the excess sand.

When you look at your treasures, remember that you had a fun, safe outing *because you obeyed your parents.*

It's Not My Fault!
Accepting responsibility for your actions

"Johnny, will you please carry this basket to the car for me?" asked Mother.

"Sure," he answered. "What's in it?"

"It's our lunch. We'll have a picnic at the zoo."

It was Saturday morning. Mother and the children had learned there was a new baby polar bear at the zoo, so they were going to make the long drive into the city to see it.

Soon they were on their way. They passed the time by singing songs and looking for license plates from other states. They were so anxious to see the baby bear!

"All right! We're almost there!" shouted Johnny as they neared the city.

In a few more minutes, Mother had driven into the parking lot at the zoo. They unloaded their picnic basket and camera, and headed for the gate.

At the gate, Mother dug around inside her purse for several minutes.

"I don't understand it," she said finally. "I *know* I had enough money in my purse yesterday, but now I don't have

278

enough to pay the admission for all of us. Do any of you know what happened to the money?"

No one answered. But Mother noticed that Elaina and Johnny were fidgeting.

"Do either of you have anything to say?" she asked, looking at Johnny and Elaina.

"Come on, Johnny," Elaina finally said, "you'd better tell. . . ."

"I did *sort* of take some money," he said. "Elaina said I should take it, so I did."

"I did not!" Elaina yelled.

"You did too!" Johnny shot back.

"That's enough shouting," said Mother. "Johnny, did you take money out of my purse?"

He looked down, then answered, "You know how you were late giving me my allowance this month?"

Mother nodded her head.

"Well," Johnny continued, "Champion came by last night for the ten dollars I borrowed from him during our vacation. You and Dad were busy talking in the kitchen, so I took the money from your purse. But I asked Elaina if she thought you would care, and she said she didn't think you would. So it's really *her* fault."

"No it's not!" said Elaina. "I thought you would tell Mommy right away!"

Mother had a sad look on her face.

"I'm disappointed in you, Johnny," she said.

"But Elaina—"

"Stop blaming your sister for what you did wrong!" Mother continued. "Accept responsibility for your mistake. You had no right to take money from my purse without asking permission. Do you think Jesus approves of this sort of thing?"

Johnny hung his head. He knew he had done wrong.

"What can we do now?" asked Joy. "Will that man let us into the zoo if we promise to give him money later?"

"No, honey," said Mother. "He needs to have the money

Let's Rehearse a Bible Verse

Being sorry in the way God wants makes a person change his heart and life. This leads to salvation.

2 Corinthians 7:10

right now. I'm afraid we'll have to go home."

Over the loud protests of her children, Mother loaded them back into the car and began the long drive home.

Check Your Head for What You've Read

1. In addition to taking money from his mother's purse, what did Johnny do that was wrong?

2. Was Johnny wrong to blame Elaina for his mistake? Why?

3. When she found out she didn't have enough money for everyone to get into the zoo, what did Mother do?

A Look Inside God's Special Book

Admitting our wrong actions and taking responsibility for them is an important part of staying right with God. Zacchaeus was a tax collector for the king. But he took more money than the king required, and kept the extra for himself. In other words, he was a cheater.

One day, Jesus came to town. Everyone wanted to see Him, including Zacchaeus. Because he was so short, Zacchaeus climbed a tree to watch for Jesus. When Jesus came by, He looked up into the tree and told Zacchaeus He wanted to go to his house! Zacchaeus admitted the wrong things he had done, and said he would pay people he had cheated *four times* as much as the amount he stole from them.

Find this story in Luke 19.

When You Pray, Day by Day
Ask God:
• to give you the courage to accept responsibility for the wrong things you do
• to help you accept the consequences of your sin gracefully—without complaining.
Thank God for giving you the desire to make the wrong things you have done right again.

Something Fun for Everyone
A responsibility is like a chore or a duty
—it's something someone expects us to do. But we don't automatically know how to be responsible—responsibility is something we must *learn*.

Have a family talk about responsibility. Prepare some snacks and lemonade for everyone, and discuss the statements below. Talk about what your parents expect of you, what God expects of you, and what you should expect of yourself.

It's my responsibility to:
• do my share of family chores
• admit the wrong things I do and try to make them right again
• be respectful of others and their ideas
• grow as a Christian in obedience and honor
• resolve conflict in a calm, respectful manner
• ask forgiveness of God and others when I do something wrong
• offer forgiveness to people who have done something wrong to me
• set a Christian example for others to follow.

Can you think of other areas of responsibility not mentioned above?
Talk about them, too.

A Birthday Surprise
Jesus changes people

Father and Elaina were just arriving home. Today was Elaina's birthday, and Elaina and her dad had gone out to lunch together–just the two of them.

"SURPRISE!" they heard as they walked into the house. It was decorated with colorful streamers and balloons. Elaina's look of amazement changed to a smile as she looked around and saw the room full of her friends.

"Happy birthday to you . . ." they all sang as Mother brought in the cake.

"Make a wish," suggested Johnny as Elaina got ready to blow out the candles.

Elaina looked around at her family and friends. So many of the people she loved were here. But she noticed that Eli Smith wasn't in the room. She knew he was shy and afraid of groups. Elaina decided to make her wish a silent prayer:

Lord, I hope that someday my friend Eli can learn to be happy around other kids. . . .

284

The room was filled with joyful chatter as everyone sat down at the table and began eating cake and ice cream. Elaina didn't even hear a quiet knock at the front door. But Mother did, and she went to answer it.

285

"H-happy b-birthday, Elaina." Eli had come after all! She turned in her chair to greet her friend and was in for an even bigger surprise—Jeremy Brown had come too!

"Hi, Elaina. Happy birthday!" Jeremy said.

Elaina smiled at her mother. She was glad Mother had remembered to invite Jeremy.

As Elaina opened her gifts, she could see that some of her friends were staring at Jeremy and whispering to one another. They must have been even more surprised than she was to see him at the party—and he had come with Eli Smith!

Everyone knew how cruel Jeremy had been to Eli during the school year. But most of Elaina's friends didn't know Eli had been helping Jeremy with his summer school homework all summer.

"Let's play Pin the Tail on the Donkey," Mother suggested after Elaina had opened all her gifts.

Eli didn't want to play the game. But before he could say no, Elaina tied the blindfold around his eyes. Jeremy guided Eli's wheelchair over to the donkey picture on the wall.

"Reach as high as you can, Eli—that's it," said Jeremy. "Now push the pin into the wall."

Everyone laughed as Eli's blindfold was removed. The donkey now had a tail growing from its knee! Tears of joy came to Elaina's eyes when she saw Eli laughing too.

The party was a great success. As everyone was leaving, Elaina overheard her friend Laura talking to another friend.

"Why is Jeremy Brown so nice all of a sudden?"

Let's Rehearse a Bible Verse

Remember this: Anyone who brings a sinner back from the wrong way will save that sinner's soul from death.

James 5:20

Laura asked. Elaina just smiled to herself.

As Jeremy pushed Eli home, he asked, "Do you think you can tell me more about Jesus now, Eli?"

Eli smiled.

"S-sure I c-can," he said.

Check Your Head for What You've Read

1. What was Elaina's biggest surprise at her birthday party?

2. What did Elaina ask God to do for Eli? Do you think God wants to help Eli?

3. What do you think caused the change that Elaina's friends noticed in Jeremy?

A Look Inside God's Special Book

The Good News about Jesus changes lives. One day, Paul and Silas were arrested for serving God. They were badly beaten and thrown into a Roman jail. The jailer didn't treat them with kindness—he put Paul and Silas deep inside the prison and put them in chains.

That night, as Paul and Silas were praying and worshiping God, a mighty earthquake broke open all the doors of the jail cells. The prisoners' chains broke too. The jailer woke up and thought the prisoners had escaped. He was so upset, he wanted to kill himself.

But Paul shouted to the jailer, "Do not hurt yourself! We are all here!" The jailer was amazed. He asked them how he could be saved, and he became a Christian that very night!

Find this story in Acts 16.

When You Pray, Day by Day
Ask God:
• to show you how to bring happiness into the life of an unhappy person
• to show you how to let Jesus' love be seen in you.
Thank God for the miracle of a life changed by the Good News of Jesus.

Something Fun for Everyone
Summer is a great time to show your friends that followers of Jesus can have just as much fun as anyone else! (Maybe *more*.)

• **Have a summertime water bash**. Summer birthdays are a good excuse to have a fun party. If you don't have any birthdays to celebrate, have a party anyway! Try some of these outdoor party activities:

• **Water-gun shootout.** Have your friends bring a squirt gun and an extra set of dry clothes. Divide up into two groups and see which team can get the other wetter! (Squirt bottles, available at many stores, are a good alternative to squirt guns.)

• **Water-balloon blast.** To get really wet, buy a couple of packages of water balloons, fill the balloons with water, and place them in buckets or pans. In a confined part of the yard—make sure boundaries are clearly marked—let everyone start throwing balloons. Anyone who has had all the water he or she wants can step over the boundary line to "safe" territory.

• **Car-wash capers**. Work can be play! Invite friends over to help you wash your parents' car. This can be a lot of wet fun, too!

Always have refreshments when you have a water bash. And try to invite friends who might not already know that being a Christian is fun.

What's Wrong with Me?
God made our bodies just right

"Good-bye, Mom. Good-bye, Joy," said Johnny as he, Father, and Elaina rode away on their bikes. They were riding to Indian Camp Creek, a small stream located a few miles from town.

Mother glanced down at Joy and noticed a sad look on her face.

"Is something wrong, honey?" she asked.

"I don't ever get to do *anything*," she said with a pout.

"What do you mean?" asked Mother.

"Johnny and Elaina always get to go on bike rides, and I don't!" she answered.

"You haven't learned to ride a two-wheeler yet," said Mother. "But you will soon. After you've had some bike-riding experience, you can go on rides with your brother and sister."

"I'll *never* learn to ride a two-wheeler," said Joy. "I can't do anything right."

"That's not true," answered Mother. "As children grow older they can do more and more things."

"But I'm not as good at swimming as some of the kids in my swimming class, and they're my age. . . ."

"Everyone learns to do things at different times, honey," said Mother. "I've noticed that you draw and color much better than many other children your age. And you're very good at cutting with scissors. Did you know that?"

Joy didn't look convinced. "Well, how come I don't have pretty brown eyes like my friend Rose?" she asked.

"You have beautiful blue eyes because that's what God gave you, honey," Mother answered. "Did you know God made you the way you are, and that He made you just right?"

Joy shook her head.

"Wait here a minute. I'll be right back," Mother said. She went in the house and returned with a Bible.

"You believe what the Bible says, don't you, Joy?"

Joy nodded her head.

"Good. Then listen to what King David wrote about God in Psalm 139: 'You made my whole being. You formed me in my mother's body. I praise you because you made me in an amazing and wonderful way. What you have done is wonderful.'"

"Did God really make me *special?*" asked Joy.

"Yes, honey, He did," Mother answered. "And when God was finished with you, you were just the way He wanted you to be. You were *wonderful.*"

Joy thought about this for a minute.

"OK, we can go in now," said Joy in her matter-of-fact way. Mother knew Joy now felt better about herself.

"Before we go in, there's something I thought we might do,"

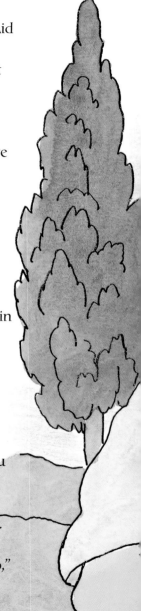

Let's Rehearse a Bible Verse

I praise you because you made me
in an amazing and wonderful way.

Psalm 139:14

Mother said. "I'd like an ice cream cone.
How about you?"
"Yes! I'm very good at eating ice cream!"
answered Joy with a grin.

Check Your Head for What You've Read

1. What did Johnny and Elaina get to do that made Joy unhappy?

2. Why wasn't Joy happy with herself?

3. What did Joy learn when Mother read from the Bible?

A Look Inside God's Special Book

God told the prophet Samuel that Jesse, a man from Bethlehem, had a son who would be the next king.

When Samuel saw Eliab, a tall and handsome son of Jesse, he thought this must be the chosen son. But God said to Samuel, "God does not see the same way people see. People look at the outside of a person, but the Lord looks at the heart."

Six more of Jesse's sons passed before Samuel, but none was the chosen son. Jesse told Samuel that his youngest son, David, was in the fields tending sheep. *David* was the chosen one! He wasn't the tallest or the oldest, but he had a good heart–he loved God.

Find this story in 1 Samuel 16.

When You Pray, Day by Day
Ask God:
• to help you be satisfied with yourself—*the way you are*
• to show you how you can have a good heart and be of service to Him.
Thank God for the wonderful way he made you.

Something Fun for Everyone
Have you ever stopped to think about what a truly marvelous creation the human body is? (Yes, yours too!) God really knows His stuff.

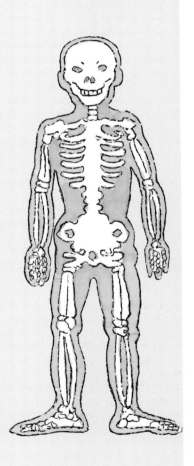

Draw a life-size bodygraph. To help you get a better idea of what kind of creation *you* are, lie down flat on your back, on a long sheet of butcher paper or freezer paper. Have a parent or friend trace around the shape of your body with a pencil. After you roll off the paper (being careful not to wrinkle or rip it), pencil in any gaps the pencil missed in the outline of your body.

Now, using an encyclopedia or other resource, draw in as many body parts as you can. (Younger children can draw such features as eyes, nose, belly button, and knees. Older children should also draw the inner parts: heart, lungs, brain, bones, muscles, and so on.)

After you complete your bodygraph, hang it up in your room and admire God's handiwork. *He did a great job when He made you!* Thank God often for making you exactly the way you are.

A Prayer for a Little Friend
Faith in God

Father, Johnny, and Elaina were out on a bicycle ride. They had stopped at Indian Camp Creek to take a short hike on the trail that ran beside the creek.

"I wonder what *that* is," said Father as he pointed at something near a big rock.

"I think it's an animal," said Elaina as they approached the object. "Yes . . . it's a baby bird!"

Father bent down over the bird. A few little brown pinfeathers stuck out on its tiny wings and tail, but otherwise the animal was just a ball of white fuzz.

"It's a baby hawk, I think. But I'm not sure it's alive, kids," Father said.

Just then the tiny bundle of fluff opened its eyes and tried to lift its head . . . but couldn't.

"It's not dead *yet!*" said Johnny. "What should we do?"

"It's almost always wrong to remove one of God's creatures from its natural surroundings," said Father.

"Fledgling hawks are often found on the ground," he continued, "but they are still being cared for by their parents. But this bird must have fallen out of its nest or tried to fly too soon. It's away from its mother and is nearly dead. Let's look

296

for worms under rocks by the creek and see if it will eat them."

Elaina stayed by the fluffy bird. In a few minutes Johnny and Father returned with several fat worms. Father tried to feed the bird a piece of one of them.

"He wants to eat it!" said Elaina. The bird tried to lift its head off the ground and open its mouth, but the effort was too much. It fell over on its side. The bird didn't have enough strength to turn back over again.

"Let's take him home and see if we can help him there," said Father. "But don't get your hopes up, kids—birds removed from the wild seldom live."

They made a bed of grass for the little bird in their empty picnic basket and began the two-mile bike ride home.

At home, Mother and Father worked hard to revive the bird. Father held it and kept its head upright while Mother squirted beef broth into its mouth with an eye dropper. They were doing what they could, but Mother and Father both knew they couldn't keep the bird alive for long without help.

"Will the birdie live?" asked Joy, her eyes wide with concern.

"We don't know," said Mother. "We need to pray that God will help us find someone who knows how to help sick birds."

"Can I pray for the baby hawk?" asked Elaina.

"Of course you can, sweetie," Mother answered.

The family bowed their heads.

"Dear Lord," she prayed, "please let the birdie live. We know you love it like we do. Help us find someone who knows how to care for sick birds. . . ."

Let's Rehearse a Bible Verse

Give your worries to the Lord. He will take care of you.
He will never let good people down.

Psalm 55: 22

After the prayer, Mother got out the phone book.
"It won't be easy to find help during the weekend, but
we've got to try," she said. She gave her children a reassuring
smile.

Check Your Head for What You've Read

1. What did Father, Elaina, and Johnny find when they were hiking along Indian Camp Creek?

2. What did the Kenton family do to try to help the little bird?

3. What did Mother say the family needed to pray for to help them save the bird?

A Look Inside God's Special Book

One day Jesus was talking to a large group of people. He said they shouldn't waste time worrying about things.

"Look at the birds in the air," Jesus said. "They don't plant or harvest or store food in barns. But your heavenly Father feeds the birds. And you know that you are worth much more than the birds. . . ."

"Look at the flowers in the field," He continued. "See how they grow. They don't work or make clothes for themselves. But I tell you that even Solomon with his riches was not dressed as beautifully as one of these flowers."

God loves and cares for us. We need to learn to trust Him. . . . We must have *faith*.

Find this story in Matthew 6.

When You Pray, Day by Day
Ask God:
• to help you believe that He wants to answer your prayers and meet your needs
• to help you make good choices when you come upon God's wild creatures.
Thank God for the many different kinds of wildlife He created.

Something Fun for Everyone
God expects us to take good care of His creation here on earth. To do this or any job well, we need to know *how* to do it.

Become "creature considerate." Begin to keep a scrapbook about God's wild animals. Find pictures of animals in magazines and glue them in your scrapbook. Borrow library books that help you learn how to deal with animals you encounter outdoors. In your notebook, write down any tips you find for appreciating or caring for wild animals. To get started, you may want to write down the following points that relate to birds you or friends may find.

• Most fledgling birds–baby birds that are getting feathers and are nearly able to fly– should be left right where you find them. They become too big for the nest, so they wind up on the ground. *That's OK.* They still need their parents' help, and the parent is probably nearby.
• Be sure to keep dogs and cats away from any bird that is no longer in its nest.
• If a baby bird (a bird that has only fuzzy feathers) falls from its nest, try to return it. (Ask for your parents' help.) You can often return a whole nest that has fallen to the ground! The bird's parents usually will come back.
• After you return a baby bird to its nest (or a nest to a tree), come back the next day to see if the bird's parents have returned. If they haven't, call your veterinarian and ask for the phone number of an *animal rehabilitator*, a person who helps sick or injured animals. They can tell you what to do.

301

Born to Be Free
Letting go of something you love

All of the Kentons wanted to help the dying baby hawk that Father, Elaina, and Johnny had found, but first they needed to figure out *how*.

"Yes, that's right," said Mother, who was talking on the phone to a veterinarian. "We've been giving the bird water and broth."

"What did the vet say?" asked Johnny eagerly after Mother hung up the phone.

"What we've been doing is fine," began Mother, "but soon we need to begin feeding the bird tiny pieces of raw meat. We also need to keep it warm with a heat lamp. So we've got lots of work to do. Who wants to help?"

All three children said they did.

By bedtime the bird's condition had improved. It could lift its head now, which it did every time anyone went near its box—because it was *always* hungry! The children started calling the bird Harry—Harry the Hawk.

That night the Kenton children prayed for their fuzzy little friend. They asked God to make him well.

303

In the morning, all three children scrambled to the laundry room, where Harry was being kept.

"How's he doing?" asked Elaina, seeing Mother and Father with the baby hawk.

"He's stronger today," answered Father. "We fed him several times during the night."

"And I see he's hungry again!" added Mother, as the little bird stretched its head up toward them with its mouth open wide.

The children took over the feeding duties during the day. Elaina carefully held the bird while Johnny fed it raw chicken with a pair of tweezers. Joy stroked its fuzzy back with her finger.

"I love our birdie," said Joy.

They had all grown fond of the helpless bird.

"Kids," said Mother that evening, "I've got some news. I just talked with a lady who takes care of sick birds. She says she will care for Harry if we take him to her in the morning."

"But, Mom!" said Johnny. "We're taking good care of him ourselves!"

"You children are doing a wonderful job," said Mother. "But this woman is a bird expert. She'll take better care of him than we can."

"Will she give him back to us?" asked Joy.

"No, honey," Mother answered. "Harry is one of God's *wild* creatures. The lady will set Harry free when he's old enough to care for himself."

"But we *love* Harry," said Elaina.

"Sometimes we need to let go of things we love," explained

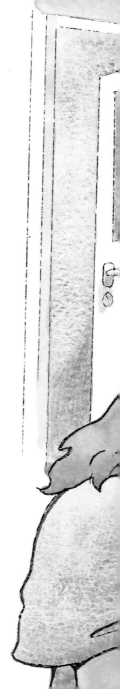

Let's Rehearse a Bible Verse

There is a time for everything.
Everything on earth has its special season.

Ecclesiastes 3:1

Mother. "Your father and I will someday have to let you children go out into the world to be on your own. That will make us sad, but it's part of God's plan."

"Mommy," said Joy, "will we remember Harry Hawk when he's gone?"

"Yes, honey," she said. "Harry has been God's gift to us for a short while. But we can love him forever."

Joy smiled as she stroked the bird's back and he opened his mouth for dinner.

305

Check Your Head for What You've Read

1. How could the Kenton children tell the baby hawk's condition was improving by the time they went to bed the first night?
2. How did the children show that they loved the bird?
3. Why couldn't the Kenton family continue to care for Harry and maybe keep him as a pet?

A Look Inside God's Special Book

A woman named Hannah was married many years without being able to have a child. She went to the Lord's Holy Tent (the tabernacle) and prayed, "Lord of heaven's armies, see how bad I feel. . . . If you will give me a son, I will give him back to you all his life."

Eli the priest saw Hannah praying. He asked God to help her. And the Lord *did* help Hannah. She became pregnant and had a son named Samuel. When the baby was old enough to eat solid food, Hannah gave him to Eli the priest to raise. Samuel would serve the Lord at the tabernacle all his life. Hannah honored her promise to God!

Find this story in 1 Samuel 1–2.

When You Pray, Day by Day

Ask God

• to help you understand why it's sometimes best to say good-bye to things we love

• to give you good memories of animals and pets that God temporarily places in your care.

Thank God when he heals animals (and people) that are sick.

Something Fun for Everyone

Life is full of changes. Sometimes we feel good about change and sometimes we don't, but it's part of life. It's a good idea for us to prepare for, and adjust to, changes.

Make a "Changes of Life Journal." Buy an inexpensive binder for standard-size notebook paper. Also buy paper (white, without lines, works best).

Next, read Ecclesiastes 3:1–8 in your Bible. This passage of Scripture contrasts various situations of life with their opposites. Using pictures you draw or clip from magazines, illustrate and write about each verse (or part of a verse) of the passage.

For example, look at verse 2. Paste or draw a picture of a baby on a left-hand page. Write, "There is a time to be born" above the picture.

Under the picture, describe the birth of someone you love. Write "There is a time to die" at the top of the *opposite* page. Paste or draw a picture (or use a photograph) of an old man or woman under the title, and write about someone special to you who has died and gone to heaven to be with Jesus.

Go all the way through the Bible passage this way, illustrating and writing about situations in life that change. Then look through your journal occasionally to remind yourself that there is a right time for everything—it's all part of God's plan.

Our Friends Need Help!

Praying for God's workers

"Mom! Dad!" yelled Johnny as he and Champion ran into the house. "Something *terrible* has happened!" Johnny was short of breath after running several blocks.

"Tell us what's wrong," said Father.

"We just talked to Kyle at the park," Johnny said, after catching his breath. "The missionaries who stayed with our family last fall have been kidnapped in Colombia!"

"The Martinez family? Kidnapped?" asked Mother in disbelief. "That's *awful*. Could Kyle have been mistaken?"

Johnny shook his head. "Kyle's dad heard it on the news. He called Pastor Halperin to be sure it was the family our church helps."

The Martinez family—Juan, Marie, and their sons José and Paul—had stayed with the Kentons when they visited their church to raise support to go to Colombia.

"I'm going to make a phone call to see if there's anything we can do to help," said Father.

"Mom," said Johnny quietly, "will José and his family be all right?" Johnny and José had become pen pals and good friends since the Martinezes' visit last fall.

308

"We can only hope and pray they will, Johnny," she answered. "Remember, God knows what is happening to the Martinez family, and He loves them very much."

Father had been talking on the phone for several minutes by now.

"Thank you, Pastor," they heard him say just before he hung up the phone.

"What did you find out, Mr. Kenton?" asked Champion.

"They were kidnapped by drug smugglers," Father answered. "The missionaries were meeting with some Colombians who are training to be pastors. The kidnappers broke in at dinner time. When they found out the Martinezes were Americans, they marched the family at gunpoint to a truck and left with them."

"Are they being held for ransom?" asked Mother.

"Not exactly. They want their leader to be released. He's a major drug smuggler who was captured and is in an American prison."

"Are the Martinezes in danger?" asked Johnny.

"Yes," Father answered, "I'm afraid they are. The kidnappers said they will kill them one by one if their leader isn't released within forty-eight hours."

"So, what can we do?" asked Johnny.

"We can pray," said Father. "Prayer is a powerful weapon. These friends need our prayers, and they need them right *now*. Johnny, go get your sisters. I want them to pray with us. Would you like to stay, Champion?"

"You guys really believe this prayer stuff works, don't you?" said Champion.

"Yes we do," answered Father.

Champion thought for a moment. "Sure—I'll stick around," he said finally. "I'd like to learn more about prayer."

Let's Rehearse a Bible Verse

So go and make followers of all people in the world.

Matthew 28:19

The Kenton family prayed as hard as they ever had that afternoon.

Check Your Head for What You've Read

1. What bad news did Johnny and Champion share with Mother and Father?
2. Were the missionaries in danger? What kind?
3. What did the Kentons do when they found out about the kidnapping? Do you think Champion believed in the power of prayer? Do *you*?

A Look Inside God's Special Book

Missionaries, people who take the Good News of Jesus to those who do not know it, have always had a dangerous job. The apostle Paul was a missionary. Paul returned to Jerusalem after traveling for several years to share the Good News about Jesus. He was falsely accused by the Jews of crimes against the Jewish Law. Paul was arrested and thrown in prison.

Because Paul was a Roman citizen, he asked to have his case tried before Caesar in Rome. So he was placed on a ship that set sail for Rome. But once the sea voyage was underway, a mighty storm destroyed the ship. However, Paul and everyone aboard swam to safety on an island. Even here the prisoner Paul told others about Jesus. He talked with and healed many people before the journey to Rome was resumed.

Find this story in Acts 27–28.

When You Pray, Day by Day
Ask God:

• to provide for and protect the missionaries who serve Him around the world

• to protect you and children you know from drugs.

Thank God for people who are sharing the Good News of Jesus with people who don't know it.

Something Fun for Everyone
Being a missionary (or the child of a missionary) can be lonely. Ask your parents if your family can help a missionary family in some special way.

Consider these ideas:

• **Become a pen pal to a missionary child.** Find out about missionaries whom your church helps. Do they have children? Write to them! You may be able to send them e-mail messages. Send pictures of you and your family. Ask them about their prayer needs.

• **Recycle news and publications**. Send news clippings and magazines you have read to missionaries. Even old news is welcome when it comes from home!

• **Have a missionary-supply ministry.** In many countries where missionaries live it can be difficult to buy toothpaste, soap, books, and many other things that we enjoy having and using in our country. Find out what these hard-to-get items are for at least one missionary family, and send them these things.

Note: What missionaries need most is to hear that you *pray* for them. They will be comforted to know you are sharing their needs with God—and this tells them how much you care.

A Miracle in Colombia
Learning that God is real

The Kenton family prayed together for the kidnapped missionaries each morning and evening.

"Any word yet about the Martinezes?" asked Father when he got home from work.

"Pastor Halperin called today," answered Mother. "He said the drug smugglers are still demanding that their leader be released from prison, or else they will kill the Martinezes. The deadline is tonight."

As the Kentons sat down that evening to have family prayer for the missionaries, the phone rang.

"Sure, Champion," said Johnny as he answered the phone. "Come on over. You'll be just in time."

Champion wanted to pray too.

"Kids," said Father after Champion arrived, "the situation still looks very bad. Thousands of people are praying for the Martinezes tonight. Let's join them."

They sat in a circle in the living room and held hands. Johnny prayed first.

"Lord, please don't let anything bad happen to my friend

314

José and his family," he prayed.

Next it was Joy's turn.

"God," she prayed, "help our friends get away from those bad men. And please, *please* don't let them lose their teddy bears."

Mother and Father smiled at Joy's heartfelt prayer. At four years of age Joy couldn't imagine what life would be like without *her* nighttime companion, Binkie Bear.

"Jesus," began Elaina, "please make sure the missionaries are being treated well."

Father prayed that the missionaries would have a chance to tell the kidnappers about Jesus. And Mother prayed that the grandparents, uncles, aunts, and cousins of the missionaries

315

wouldn't give up hope.

After the prayer, the children went out to the backyard to play volleyball. Johnny and Joy were on one team, Champion and Elaina on the other. Johnny had just smashed the ball over the net when Mother called him to the phone.

"Hello?" Johnny said into the telephone receiver. Johnny's eyes suddenly got wide. "José? José Martinez? Is it really you?" he asked.

Mother quickly called the other children in from the backyard.

"They're safe!" yelled Johnny jubilantly as he hung up the phone. "They've been freed and they're calling their friends to tell them!"

"What happened, Johnny?" asked Mother.

"José said they were very frightened when the deadline passed and some men blindfolded them and loaded them all into a van. But the next thing they knew, they had been left on a street corner a couple of blocks away from the American embassy!"

"God is very good, kids," said Father. The children were laughing and jumping up and down. All but Champion. He had a tear rolling down his cheek.

"What's wrong, Champion?" asked Mother.

"God *did* do this, didn't He?" said Champion.

"Yes, He did," answered Mother.

"I guess I never really believed God was real," Champion said. "But I do now. Do . . . do you think *I* can become a Christian?"

"Of course you can," said Father. "If you'd like, we can sit

Let's Rehearse a Bible Verse

Believe in the Lord Jesus and you will be saved.

Acts 16:31

down and talk about it right now."

Johnny had never seen such a big smile on his friend's face as they all sat down to talk.

317

Check Your Head for What You've Read

1. Why did Champion ask Johnny if he could come over to the Kentons' house?
2. Were the Kentons the only people praying for the safety of the missionaries?
3. What was the special decision Champion made that night?

A Look Inside God's Special Book

The Pharisees of Jesus' day complained about Jesus. They said, "Look! This man welcomes sinners and even eats with them!" So Jesus told a story that He hoped would help people understand *why* He spent so much time with sinners.

Jesus said that if a woman had ten silver coins and lost one of them, she would carefully look for the lost coin until she finds it. "And when she finds it," said Jesus, "she will call her friends and neighbors and say, 'Be happy with me because I have found the coin that I lost!'" Jesus said that in the same way, the angels of heaven rejoice when even one sinner turns his heart toward God.

Find this story in Luke 15.

When You Pray, Day by Day

Ask God:

• to help you believe in Him so that you will be saved
• to give you opportunities to tell others about Jesus.

Thank God for the gift of prayer that lets us talk to our Creator in heaven.

Something Fun for Everyone

We can live with God in heaven forever because Jesus paid the price for our sins by dying on the cross. Christ's death makes it possible for us to receive the free gift of salvation.

Take a quiz about salvation. It's easy to become confused by what it means to receive the gift of salvation. The true or false quiz following this paragraph may clear up some confusion for you.

1. If I faithfully attend church every Sunday (plus any other services available during the week), I will be saved. _____ (True or false?)
2. If I unselfishly give to the church, to orphans and widows, and to the homeless, I will be saved. _____ (True or false?)
3. If I do my best to obey all of the Ten Commandments, I will be saved. _____ (True or false?)
4. If I always try to help other people, and to not hurt them, I will be saved. _____ (True or false?)
5. If I read the Bible, memorize lots of Scripture verses, and pray all the time, I will be saved. _____ (True or false?)

Did you guess that the answer to all the questions above is false? It's good to go to church, read the Bible, and do many of the things mentioned above, but doing these things can't save a person. God's gift of salvation is free—it can't be earned. The only way we can receive salvation is by believing in Jesus and accepting Him as our Lord. (Read 1 John 1:9; Romans 6:23; Ephesians 2:8–10; Isaiah 64:6; John 3:3; and Titus 3:5.)

INDEX TO TOPICS AND STORIES

Where to find the themes, subjects, and Bible characters and stories featured in *Beginning with God. Bible stories and characters are in italic type.*